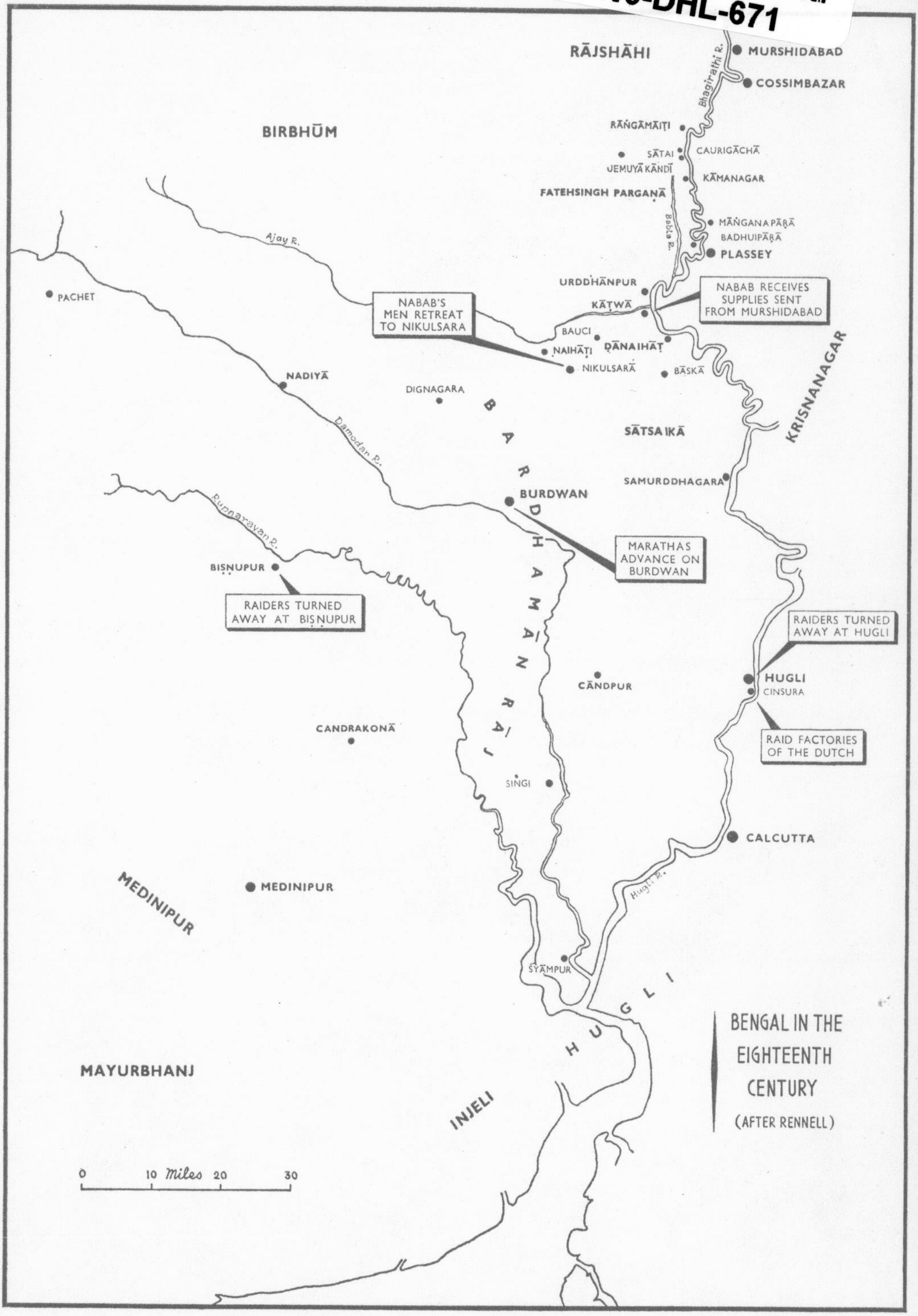
RĀJSHĀHI
MURSHIDABAD
COSSIMBAZAR
Bhagirathi R.
BIRBHŪM
RĀNGĀMĀIṬI
SĀTAI
CAURIGĀCHĀ
JEMUYĀ KĀNDĪ
KĀMANAGAR
FATEHSINGH PARGANĀ
Babla R.
MĀNGANA PĀṚĀ
BADHUIPĀṚĀ
PLASSEY
Ajay R.
PACHET
URDDHANPUR
KĀTWĀ
NABAB RECEIVES SUPPLIES SENT FROM MURSHIDABAD
NABAB'S MEN RETREAT TO NIKULSARA
BAUCI
NAIHĀṬI
ḌĀNAIHĀṬ
NIKULSARĀ
BĀSKĀ
KRISNANAGAR
NADIYĀ
DIGNAGARA
Damodar R.
SĀTSAIKĀ
SAMURDDHAGARA
BARDHAMĀN RĀJ
BURDWAN
Rupnarayan R.
MARATHAS ADVANCE ON BURDWAN
BISNUPUR
RAIDERS TURNED AWAY AT BISNUPUR
RAIDERS TURNED AWAY AT HUGLI
HUGLI
CINSURA
CĀNDPUR
CANDRAKONĀ
RAID FACTORIES OF THE DUTCH
SINGI
CALCUTTA
MEDINIPUR
MEDINIPUR
Hugli R.
SYĀMPUR
HUGLI
BENGAL IN THE EIGHTEENTH CENTURY (AFTER RENNELL)
MAYURBHANJ
INJELI
0 10 Miles 20 30

THE MAHĀRĀSHṬA PURĀṆA

The Mahārāshṭa Purāṇa

An Eighteenth-Century Bengali Historical Text

translated, annotated, and with an introduction
by Edward C. Dimock, Jr., and Pratul Chandra Gupta

Published for The Association for Asian Studies

EAST-WEST CENTER PRESS · HONOLULU

Publication of this study has been made possible by a generous grant to the Association for Asian Studies by the Ford Foundation

HONOLULU, HAWAII

L. C. Card: 64–63437

Printed in the United States of America

PREFACE

THE RESEARCH REPRESENTED by this little book was begun in the summer of 1959 by Edward Dimock, and continued during the autumn of 1960 by Edward Dimock and Pratul Chandra Gupta, when both authors were at the University of Chicago. Although of course the authors take full responsibility for the accuracy of their research and translation, they are greatly indebted to various scholars and other individuals for assistance and advice given at various points in the preparation of the manuscript for publication.

First and foremost, we should like to extend our thanks to Maureen L. P. Patterson, Bibliographer of the Southern Asian Studies program of the University of Chicago, for part of the Introduction relating to the Mahārāshtrian background and for her bibliographical help and suggestions in regard to the history of Mahārāshtra in the eighteenth century; to Professor Sukumar Sen, Khaira Professor of Indian Linguistics and Phonetics at the University of Calcutta, for his help in deciphering and interpreting many obscurities of language in the text itself; and to Professor Daniel H. H. Ingalls of Harvard University, for reading a draft of the book and helping arrange for its publication. Our thanks also go to the Registrar of the University of Calcutta and to Professor Shashibhushan Dasgupta, Professor of Bengali Language and Literature, for making accessible to us the manuscript of the text, which is deposited in the Manuscript Library of the Bengali Department of that University; to Miss Judith Aronson, Administrative Assistant of the South Asian Languages Program of the University of Chicago, and Mrs. Richard B. Martin, for their help in preparing the manuscript for publication; to Mr. Ronald Inden and Mr.

Wayne Kilpatrick, graduate students in Bengali at the University of Chicago, for checking the accuracy of the transcription against the manuscript; to Dr. Ralph W. Nicholas of Michigan State University for the maps, and Miss Mary Carmen Lynn of the University of Chicago for preparation of the indices.

Our indebtedness to those scholars to whose published works we have had occasion to refer is recorded in the notes to the Introduction and the text itself.

Edward C. Dimock, Jr.
Chicago, 1961

Pratul Chandra Gupta
Calcutta, 1961

CONTENTS

THE MANUSCRIPT OF THE MAHĀRĀSHṬA PURĀṆA

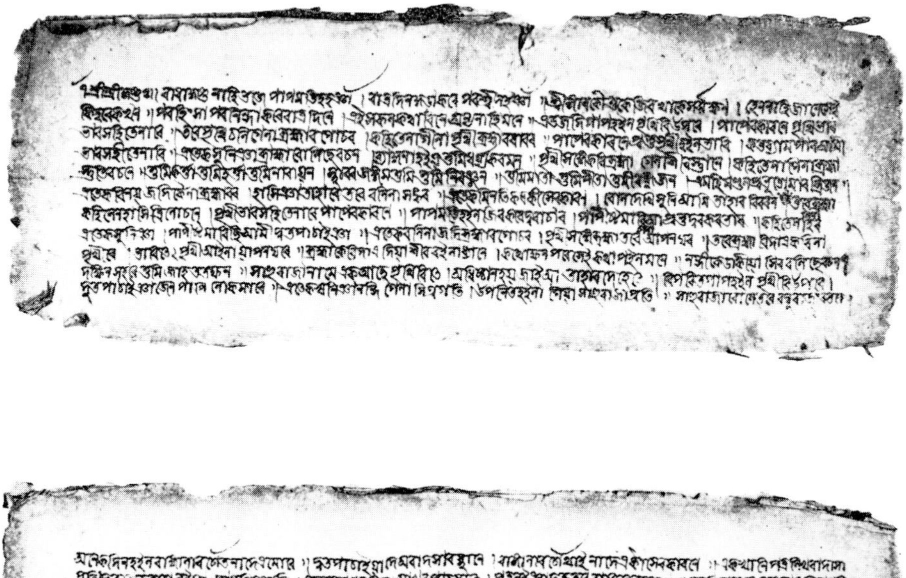

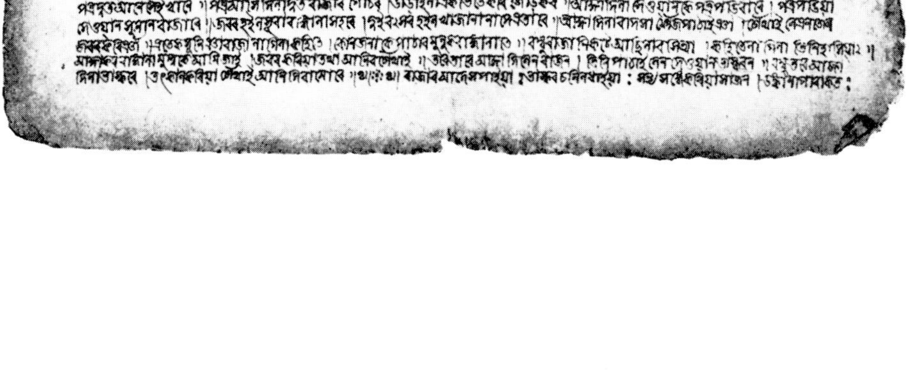

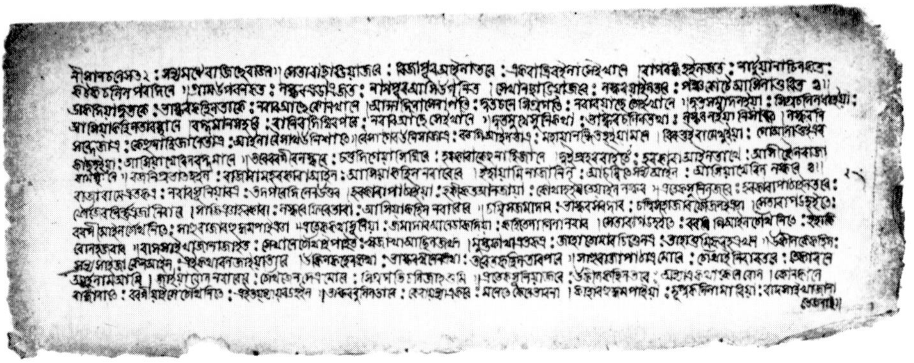

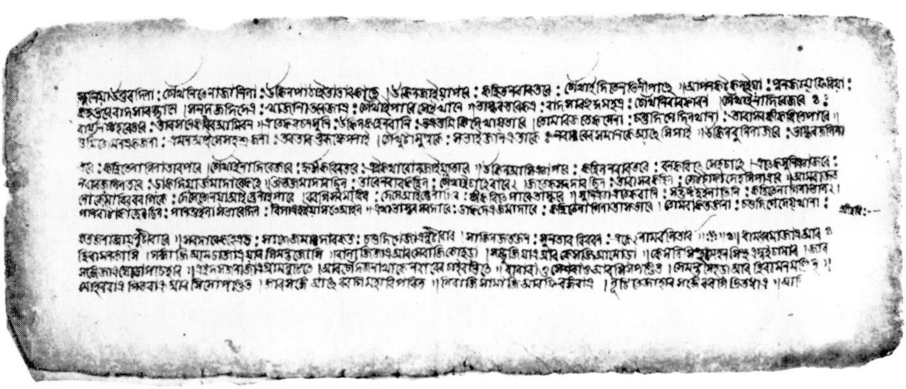

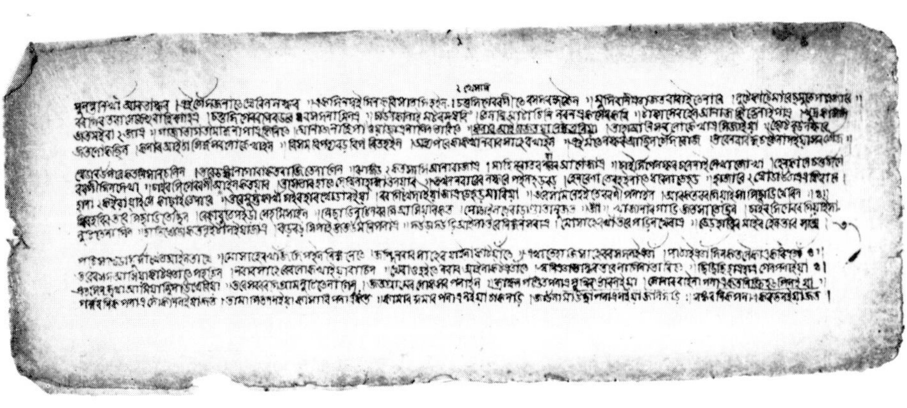

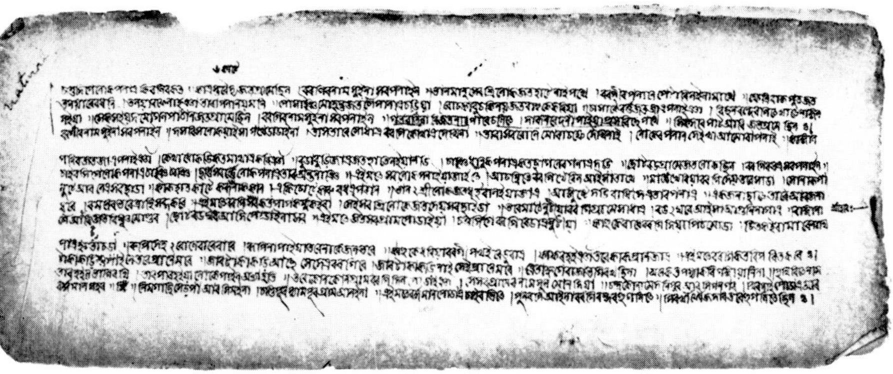

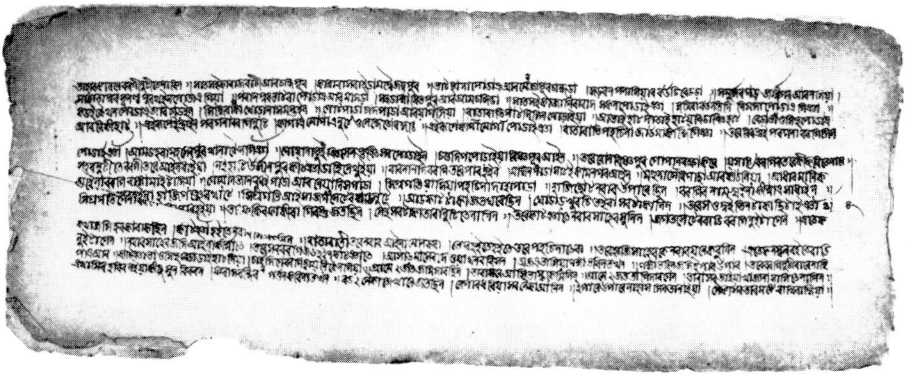

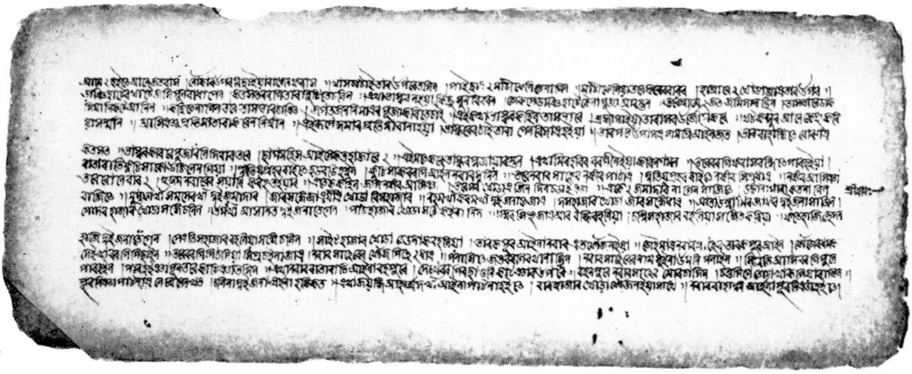

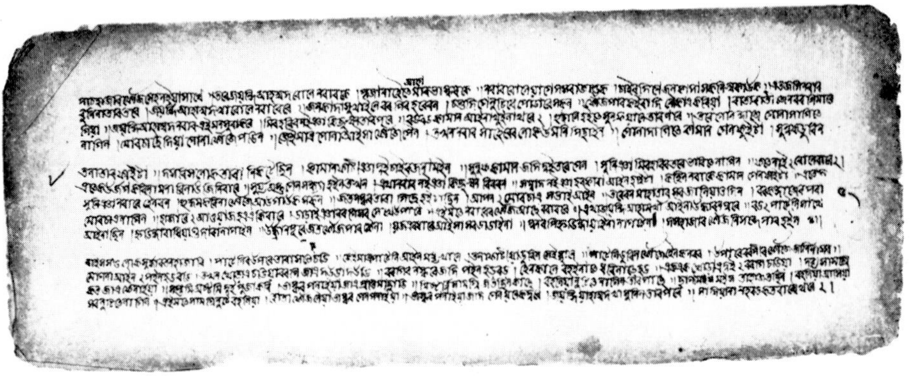

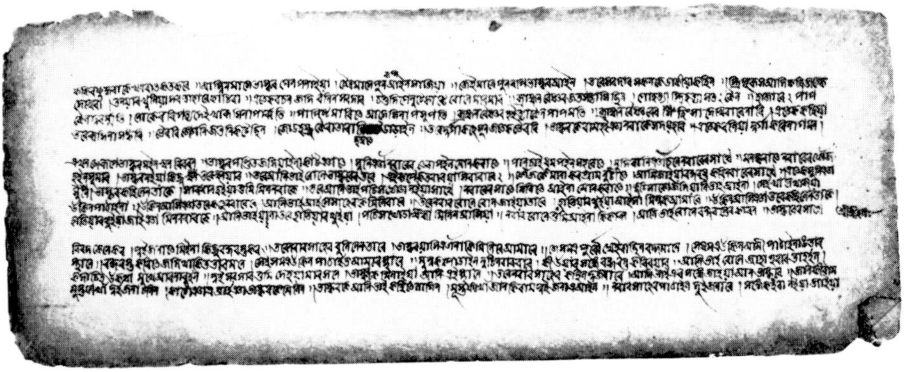

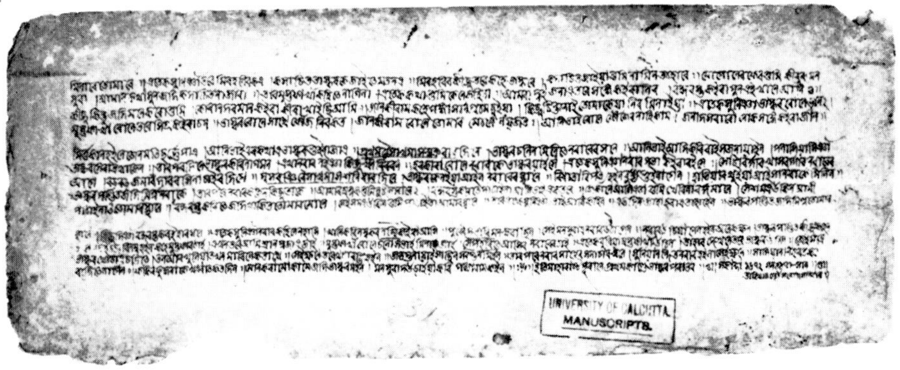
UNIVERSITY OF CALCUTTA
MANUSCRIPTS.

TRANSLITERATION AND TRANSLATION

IN THE TRANSLATION of the text, Bengali terms are preserved wherever adequate English translations have not been found, and the terms are explained in the footnotes. In such cases, as well as throughout the transliteration of the text itself, we have tried to use the system of transliteration accepted by most scholars for the Sanskritic languages. However, Bengali is peculiar among the Sanskritic languages in certain respects. For example, the labio-dental spirant (represented by the letter *v*) does not occur in Bengali. Where *v* occurs in Sanskrit, *b* occurs in Bengali; therefore, *b* has been used in our transliteration, except where a cluster of consonant and *v* occurs or where the reference is to a Sanskrit, not a Bengali, word. Furthermore, the pronunciation of the Bengali symbol usually transliterated by *y*, when it occurs medially in a word, depends upon the vowel which precedes it. If this symbol is preceded by *o* or *u*, and sometimes when it is preceded by *a* ([ɔ]), it is pronounced as *w*; we have thus indicated this symbol in our transliteration when it occurs in the above positions as (*w*). Elsewhere, we have tried to be consistent with custom, even to the extent of preserving sentence final -a, which is not pronounced in reading Bengali poetry.

A remark or two might be made about the scribal peculiarities of the manuscript, which have some bearing on our transliteration of the text. The scribe's hand does not always distinguish between the characters represented in our transliteration by *l* and *n*, nor does he usually distinguish between what we have represented as *b* and *r*. The *l-n* variation may be indicative of dialect or merely of the similarity of the characters in Bengali script; the *b-r* variation is clearly scribal peculiarity. In any case, in both situations we have read the variant appropriate to the context, and have represented it as such in our transliteration.

In some cases, Bengali dialectical or other nonstandard forms occur in the manuscript of the text. Such are given in our translation in the form in which they occur in the manuscript, with the more standard form being given in the notes wherever possible. For example, the form *ukil* will be left as such in our translation, with a note which refers to the more standard form *vakil*.

Place names are given in the translation in the form in which they occur in the text, with the Anglicized form (where possible) either in following brackets or in the notes, e. g., Bardhamān [Burdwan], Palāsi [Plassey]. In the Introduction to the text, however, place names are given throughout in Anglicized form, e. g., Vishnupur.

We have tried to make the translation of the text as accurate as readability in English will allow. In some places, the manuscript is indecipherable due to mutilation or faded ink, or the reading is unclear for some other reason. Such places, as well as those at which the manuscript reading is at variance with the printed text, are indicated in the notes.

INTRODUCTION

MAHĀRĀSHṬA PURĀṆA (or *Mahārāshtra Purāṇa,* as it is sometimes called) is the title of an eighteenth-century Bengali manuscript first discovered about 60 years ago. It was brought to light in an exhibition in 1904 in the town of Mymensingh in East Bengal, now East Pakistan. The manuscript contains a long narrative poem of 716 lines, telling of the Maratha [1] invasions of Bengal in the middle of the 18th century.

BACKGROUND

The Maratha invasions of Bengal, which might more accurately be described as a series of raids, began in April, 1742, when some twenty-five thousand horsemen sent by Rāghuji Bhonsle, Maratha ruler of Nagpur, suddenly appeared in Bengal under their leader Bhāskar Pant Kolhatkar, commonly known in Bengal as Bhāskara Paṇḍit, and demanded the *cauth,* traditionally the fourth part of the revenue of the province (though in actuality often less).[2]

1. Here and throughout the Introduction, the term "Maratha" is not used in its technical reference to a single caste of Mahārāshtra, but is used to denote persons of all castes who speak the Marathi language. See Irawati Karve, *Kinship Organization of India* (Poona: Deccan College, 1953), p. 155 n.
2. On the matter of *cauth,* J. N. Das Gupta ("An Eighteenth Century Bengali Manuscript," in the *Calcutta Review* for April, 1917, pp. 164–165) quotes William Bolts, *Considerations on Indian Affairs* (printed for J. Almon et al.: London, 1772, pp. 7–8), to the following effect:

"There are several nations in India, now living under distinct governments of their own, who never were subdued by the Moguls, though indeed most of them at times have been their tributaries. They, however, were never able to make the Marahtahs either their subjects or tributaries.

"These people are governed by an aristocracy of Rajahs of the Hindoo

In 1742, the Mughal Empire was falling to pieces. Muhammad Shāh, Emperor of Delhi, exercised ineffective control over the outlying provinces; Bengal (which then included Bihar and Orissa) had become semi-independent under the usurper 'Alivardi Khān, the Nawāb, or governor, who had revolted against Nawāb Sarfarāz Khān and slain him in battle.[3]

When the Marathas struck, in 1742, 'Alivardi Khān, Nawāb of Bengal, was returning to his capital, Murshidabad, from Orissa, where he had been campaigning against some rebels; he was surprised and surrounded by the Maratha cavalry on the outskirts of the city of Burdwan, about 70 miles west of Calcutta. 'Alivardi succeeded in beating them off. But the Maratha raids became an annual affair, and in 1744 the exasperated Nawāb treacherously summoned Bhāskara Paṇḍit to a conference and had him murdered.

religion, for they imposed tributes on most of their neighbors; and at last they even obliged the famous Mogul Aurangzebe to submit to the mortifying and dishonourable terms of paying them a *chout*, or annual tribute of the fourth part of the revenues of the Deckhan; so that it might be said, the Emperor thereby acknowledged . . . their joint right of sovereignty with him over those provinces that produced the revenues out of which the *chout* was paid.

" This *chout* or tribute was continued to be received by the Marahtahs from the Mogul even long after the revenues of the Deckhan Provinces had ceased to be paid into the royal treasury at Dehly: for in the year 1740, when the deputies of the Sahoo Rajah (King of Sittarah) arrived as usual at Dehly to receive the *chout*, they were told by the Mogul's ministry that Nader Shah had lately so exhausted the treasury, that the Emperor was rendered utterly incapable of satisfying their demands, the more especially as the revenues of the Bengal provinces had been withheld from the year 1738 by the rebellion of Allaverdy Khawn, who in conjunction with his brother Hajee Ahmed, had usurped the Government of that Subahdary, they requesting at the same time that the deputies would entreat their master, in the Emperor's name, to send any army of sufficient force to exact the amount of the *chout* that was due to them. . . ."

Charles Stewart's *History of Bengal* (London, 1813; 2nd ed., Calcutta: Bangabasi Office, 1910), on the other hand, tells us that 'Alivardi felt that collection of the *cauth* was a less potent reason for the invasion than was the jealousy of the Nizām of Hyderabad, who was wary of the rising power of Bengal, and therefore instigated the invasion.

3. 'Alivardi Khān had risen from a low position in the service of the Nawāb Shujā-ud-din Khān to the deputyship in Bihar. Upon Shujā's death, his son Sarfarāz Khān became Nawāb; 'Alivardi rose in revolt against him and killed him. See Karam 'Ali, " Muzaffar Nāmah," in Jadunath Sarkar, *Bengal Nawābs* (Calcutta: Asiatic Society, 1952), pp. 11 ff.

This, however, did not put an end to the Maratha incursions. These continued until May of 1751, when 'Alivardi signed a treaty with Rāghuji Bhonsle, by which he forfeited Orissa and promised, among other things, to pay annually a sum of twelve lakhs [4] of rupees as *cauth*.

THE TEXT AND ITS AUTHORSHIP

The *Mahārāshṭa Purāṇa* covers only the early part of this story, leading up to and including the murder of Bhāskara. It was probably the poet's intention to write a complete account of the Maratha invasions of Bengal, for the closing line of the manuscript which we have reads: "Thus ends the first part of the *Mahārāṣṭa Purāṇa*, [called] *Bhāskara-parābhaba* ["The Defeat of Bhāskara"]." Whether or not the poet ever finished his narrative, of which only this one part survives, or whether this was all he ever wrote, is still unknown. The latter possibility seems more likely. The manuscript of the work preserved in the Bengali Department of the University of Calcutta seems to be the only extant one.

The name of the poet, which appears in the text, is Gaṅgarām. There has been some speculation as to his identity, but nothing really is known of him.[5] It does seem, from the intense realism of some of his descriptions, that he was in some way close to the events which surrounded the Maratha invasions, but this is really all that can be said. There is a date given in the manuscript itself: "*śonibar* [Saturday], the 14th of *pouṣ* [December-January], *saka* 1672, *sala* 1158 [A.D. 1751–1752]." This may be either the date when the scribe finished his copy of the manuscript, or it may be the date of its composition. Again, the latter possibility seems likely. It has been suggested that the handwriting is the author's own, but there is no substantial evidence for such a contention; it is no more than a surmise.

Not only does the poet appear to have personal knowledge of the Maratha depredations, but he seems also to be familiar with

4. One lakh = 100,000.
5. The Bengali scholar Rameścandra Bandyopādhyāya feels that this Gaṅgarām might be the poet Gaṅgārām Datta, but this seems to be no more than a guess. See Sukumār Sen, *Bāṅgālā sāhityer itihāsa* (Calcutta: Modern Book Agency, 1948. 2nd edition), vol. I, pp. 675 and 856.

the country which they visited—those districts west of the Hughli River in West Bengal. On the basis of these facts, plus the fact that he thought that certain verb forms found in the manuscript were peculiar to West Bengal, Byomakesh Mustafi, who first edited the manuscript and published it in the *Sāhitya pariṣad patrikā*,[6] unhesitatingly called Gaṅgārām "a native of Rāṛha [i. e., West Bengal]."[7] This view was, however, challenged by Kedarnāth Majumdār, who believed that he had found in a village in Mymensingh District in East Bengal several other works composed by Gaṅgārām; he claimed that Gaṅgārām's ancestors had been residents of that village for at least three generations. He said also that the verb forms, on which Byomakesh Mustafi had based most of his conclusions about Gaṅgārām, were not peculiar to West Bengal, but were current in other parts of the province as well.[8] It might be added that Kedarnāth Majumdār's opinion in the latter respect is supported by the use in the manuscript of many phrases and idioms common in East Bengal dialects.[9]

6. The journal of the Baṅgiya sāhitya pariṣad, Calcutta; the text is published in vol. 13, B. S. 1314 (A. D. 1908).
7. P. 207. The linguistic argument is essentially this:
   Many non-finite verbal forms throughout the text have /-ñā/ final. According to Mustafi, the type of nasalization which this unusual orthography represents is a dialectal peculiarity of Burdwan, Bankura, and Birbhum districts—the districts which bore the brunt of the Maratha invasions (pp. 207-208). In regard to this orthographic use of the palatal nasal symbol, see Sukumār Sen. *Bhāsār itibrtta* (Burdwan: *Sāhitya sabhā*, 1957), p. 231. G. A. Grierson (*Linguistic Survey of India*, Calcutta: Office of the Superintendent of Government Printing, vol. 5 (1903), p. 71) also finds that the Manbhum (now in eastern Bihar) district dialect is "fond of nazalising the final vowel of the verb."
8. *Sāhitya pariṣad patrikā*, B. S. 1315 (A. D. 1909), part 4, pp. 249-253. The other side of the linguistic argument is that such non-finite verb forms with nasalized final as are mentioned above are not used consistently throughout the text. The participial form of the stem /dekh-/, "see," occurs as /dekhiyā, dekhiñā, deikhyā, and deikhā/. The last two are almost certainly East Bengal forms; Grierson (*op. cit.*, pp. 205, 209) finds the form /deikhā/ in the Dacca dialect and similar forms (e.g., /kairyā/ for the more standard /kariyā/, "doing") in Mymensingh. An argument based upon the orthographic use of the dental sibilant for all three (orthographic) sibilant sounds is similarly inconclusive. Some Bengali dialects of the east have only the dental sibilant, but this is also true for some dialects of the west (Grierson, *op. cit.*, p. 128).
9. For example, near the end of the text, *laghyi kairā āsi*, "I am going out to urinate," is a polite Bengali dialectal form.

REFERENCES TO THE ORIGIN AND NATURE OF THE MARATHA RAIDS

The *Mahārāshṭa Purāṇa* is not the first account of the Maratha raids in Bengal. There exists an earlier Sanskrit work, the *Citracampū*, written in 1744 by Vāṇeśvara Vidyālaṅkāra, the court poet of the Mahārājā of Burdwan. This text gives only a vague and conventional account of the invasion; the author was far more concerned with poetic effects than with historical details. There is, however, one verse which illustrates clearly the characteristics of the Maratha horsemen and the terror which they spread among the people:

[They] travel a hundred *yojanas* [10] in one day, killing
the unarmed and submissive, women and children,
stealing whatever they find, abducting virtuous women;
and in the face of battle, quickly and by stealth they escape to
another country
on their swift horses—which is their chief strength.[11]

It is somewhat surprising that in spite of the excitement and terror which the Maratha raids spread in Bengal, they are not often mentioned in contemporary Bengali literature. Apart from the *Mahārāshṭa Purāṇa*, one finds an occasional nursery rhyme about the coming of the *bargis*,[12] or an occasional ballad, such as the one current in Vishnupur, in which the local deity himself fires the cannon and saves the town from the Marathas.[13] But one would search in vain for good accounts of the Maratha raids in the writings of two famous poets contemporary with them—Rāmprasād Sen (1718?–1775?) and Bhāratcandra Rāy (1712–1760).

Rāmprasād lived on the east bank of the Hughli near Calcutta,

10. One *yojana* is about eight miles; clearly the reference is not literal here.
11. Vāṇeśvara Vidyālaṅkāra, *Citracampū*, edited by Rāmcaraṇ Cakravarti, (Benares: Harakumar Chakravarti, 1940), p. 13.
12. The term "*bargi*" (/borgi/) is the term used in the *Mahārāshṭa Purāṇa*, and still used today, as a general term for the Maratha soldiery. It was originally a Persian military term (*bargir*) denoting a cavalryman whose horse was the property of someone else. See Surendranath Sen, *Military System of the Marathas* (Calcutta: Orient Longmans, 1958), p. 4. One of the rhymes in question will be quoted below.
13. The ballad referred to is given as an appendix to the text.

and must have been familiar with stories of the Marathas. But Rāmprasād was primarily a religious poet; perhaps he did not feel this secular matter a suitable subject for his poetry. Bhāratcandra, on the other hand, did not ignore the Marathas entirely. In the prologue to his famous trilogy *Annadāmaṅgal*, he writes:

The dream which the Maratha king saw made him angry;
Rāghuji Bhonsle sent Bhāskara Paṇḍit,
and with him an army of men, ugly and fierce—
troopers from Mahārāshtra, Saurāshtra [Surat and surrounding areas], and other places.
They robbed the people of Bengal and made them beggars,
and making bridges of boats they crossed the Ganges.[14]

But except in these few lines and one more brief reference to their devastation of Bhubaneśvar in Orissa, Bhāratcandra never referred to the Marathas again. This is all the more surprising, for, unlike Rāmprasād, Bhāratcandra was very much a secular poet, and came from the part of West Bengal devastated by the Marathas (Burdwan).[15] It is even said that in his younger days he lived a while under the protection of a Maratha cavalry officer who saved him from the anger of the Mahārājā of Burdwan.[16] He had, therefore, better opportunity than most of his contemporaries to know the Marathas. Why he so ignores them remains a mystery.

Like Bhāratcandra, Gaṅgārām looked upon the Maratha incursions as a punishment for sin, though the sin is not the same to both writers. Bhāratcandra imagined the incursions to be brought about by the misconduct of 'Alivardi's army at Bhubaneśvar, where 'Alivardi was fighting rebels. Bhubaneśvar is a holy place of pil-

14. *Bhāratcandra-granthābalī*, edited by Brajendranāth Bandyopādhyāya and Sajanikānta Dās (Calcutta: Sāhitya pariṣad, B.S. 1357, A.D. 1950), pp. 13-14. The second line (*bargirājā . . . pāṭhāila rāghurājā bhāskara paṇḍit/*) might also read, "The Maratha king sent Rāghuji and Bhāskara Paṇḍit." Rāghuji did go to Bengal, though after Bhāskara's death.

15. He was born in the village of Pandua in the Bhursut area of Burdwan, and at various later phases of his life lived in a village near Hughli and in the city of Chandarnagar (Sukumār Sen. *History of Bengali Literature*, New Delhi: Sahitya Akademi, 1960), p. 165.

16. See the account of Iśvaracandra Gupta, quoted in *Bhāratcandra-granthābalī*, introduction, p. 18.

grimage associated with Śiva and Durgā, and Bhāracandra's imagination runs thus:

After the desecration of the holy place by the Nawāb 'Alivardi's troops, Śiva's attendant Nandi became violently angry, and was about to destroy the universe. He was prevented from doing so by Śiva, who directed him to appear in the dream referred to in the verse above to the Maratha king Sāhu at Sātārā, who would then set forth to punish the Nawāb. Thus, the desecration of Bhubaneśvar by the "sinful" 'Alivardi brought on the Maratha invasion, and life in Bengal and Bihar "became like hell." Why should innocent people suffer because of the sin of 'Alivardi's troops? Bhāratcandra had an answer to that—"When the city burns, does the temple escape?"[17]

Gaṅgārām, however, does not put the blame on 'Alivardi's army. He says: "Once there was a time when the people of the earth were filled with sin. There was no worship of Rādhā and Kṛṣṇa, and day and night the people took their pleasure with the wives of others. The days were passed in amorous sport and love-making, and in abusing others and doing injury to them." The burden of this sin became too heavy for the Earth; she appealed to Brahmā, who asked Śiva to "strike down these evil people, and rid Earth of her burden." So the Marathas struck them down.

ORIGINS OF THE MARATHA RAIDS

There were more worldly reasons for the raids of the Marathas, and these might be outlined at this point.

Various accounts of these events can be found in some of the contemporary or nearly contemporary Persian Chronicles. The most detailed account is in the *Siyār-ul-Mutākherīn* ("A Review of Our Own Times"), written by Ghulām Hussain Khān, who described himself as "an actor or spectator" in the events which he narrates.

Ghulām Hussain begins his history at the death of Aurangzeb in 1707. Since he himself was not born until 1727-28, clearly he could not have witnessed or acted in the earlier events of his narrative. At the time of the Maratha raids, however, he was a young

17. *Ibid.*, p. 13.

man, and as his father was a high government official, it was possible for him to secure accurate information. About the origins of the Maratha incursions into Bengal, he states that Rāghuji Bhonsle was " a prince related to the Rājā Sāhu and one of the most renowned commanders in the Marhatta Empire. This Prince, either instigated by Nizām-ul-Mulk,[18] or prompted by what he knew of the weakness of the Empire, undertook to make an irruption into the Kingdom of Bengal. His views were either to make a conquest of it, or at least to establish in it contributions to the full amount of *cauth*, i. e., one quarter of the revenue, an odious yoke that had become established in many countries of Hindoostan and Deccan, but from which Bengal had yet remained entirely free. For this purpose he made a choice of his own Prime Minister Bhāskar Pandit and gave him the command of an army of twenty-five thousand horse, which renown has swelled to forty thousand, and that army had passed with ease to the mountainous country and difficult passes. . . . nobody ever thought of opposing their passage." [19]

In another Persian Chronicle, the *Muzaffar Nāmah* of Karam 'Ali, there is a fairly complete account of the Maratha invasions. Karam 'Ali was a " news writer " in the Burdwan area during the administration of a former Nawāb, Shujā Khān (1726-1739), and later was appointed by 'Alivardi to the post of *faujdār* [20] in north Bengal. His view of the origins of the Maratha incursions was that Rastam Jang, the deputy-governor of Orissa, who had no love for 'Alivardi, went to the Deccan and " waited on Nizām-ul-Mulk and begged him for aid. . . . the latter out of his practical knowledge

18. Asāf Jāh Nizām-ul-Mulk, the Regulator of the Empire, who governed the vice-royalty of the Deccan in near-independence from Delhi, eventually proclaiming it a hereditary possession of his family. In 1724 he moved to Hyderabad, assuming authority in the Carnatic also.

19. Ghulām Hussain Khān, *Siyār-ul-Mutākherīn* (English translation, Calcutta: The Asiatic Society, 1901-1902, 4 vols.), vol. I, pp. 376-377.

20. Ramesh Chandra Majumdar, et al., *Advanced History of India* (London; Macmillan, 1950), p. 558: " In the districts or sarkars, law and order were maintained usually by officers like the Faujdars. The faujdar, as his name suggests, was only the commander of a military force stationed in the country. He had to put down smaller rebellions, disperse or arrest robber gangs, take cognizance of all violent crimes, and make demonstrations of force to overawe opposition to the revenue authorities, or the criminal judge, or the censor."

sent a secret hint to the Marathas, inciting them with greed for the money and property of Bengal." [21]

Yusuf 'Ali, the author of the *Āhwāl-i-Mahābat Jang*, and the son-in-law of the Nawāb Sarfarāz Khān, whom 'Alivardi had deposed, also refers to the instigation of Nizām-ul-Mulk: "Rāghuji Bhonsle . . . outwardly on seeing the weakness of the sultani government but inwardly at the instigation of Nizām-ul-Mulk Asāf Jāh with the object of conquering the Kingdom of Bengal if possible, or else for exacting the *cauth* which was customary in all the (other) provinces of Hind, but from which Bengal had been free, sent Bhāskar Pandit, one of his noted chiefs, with nearly 20,000 horse to Bengal." [22]

Other chroniclers of the period, for example Salimullah, author of the *Tārikh-i-Bangāla*, did not mention this role played by Nizām-ul-Mulk or the encouragement given Rāghuji Bhonsle by the conditions at Delhi. Salimullah does, however, give details of the campaigns themselves, and we shall have occasion to refer to his narrative in the notes to the text.

Apart from the Persian Chronicles, there are various contemporary English writers who supply us with some details of the Maratha invasions. Although William Watts does not refer to them in his *Memoirs*, both J. Z. Holwell and Luke Scrafton supply us with accounts of varying accuracy and value.

Holwell, who is best known for his description of the Black Hole of Calcutta,[23] describes the Maratha invasions in detail. Although he wrote that during his thirty-year residence in Bengal he "employed his leisure hours" in collecting materials "relative to the transactions, revolutions, and occurrences of that invaluable country" [24] in regard to 'Alivardi Khān and his successor Sirāj-ud-daulah, there is no other English writer of the time whose words carry less authority. Holwell disliked 'Alivardi so much that he rarely referred to him by name, but nearly always called him "the usurper." He

21. Sarkar, *Bengal Nawābs*, p. 28.

22. *Ibid.*, p. 96.

23. J. Z. Holwell, *India Tract* (London: printed for T. Becket, 1764).

24. J. Z. Holwell, *Interesting Historical Events Relative to the Province of Bengal and the Empire of Indostan* (London: printed for T. Becket and P. A. De Hondt, 1766-1771), p. 3.

also circulated the story that 'Alivardi never received the *farmān* or letters-patent from the Emperor of Delhi which would have made his position as Nawāb legal. According to Holwell, the *farmān* " published by beat of drum " and " industriously circulated " by the Seths, the state bankers, was not genuine. The Seths, he said, " could always cook up a *phirmand* [*farmān*] from the court whenever it was wanted." [25] Holwell's statement, however, is not supported by other contemporary historians. Karam 'Ali says that 'Alivardi met the Emperor's agent at Rajmahal, and that the agent presented him with a royal *khilat* [26] and " congratulated him." [27] Yusuf 'Ali also admits that 'Alivardi " received from the Emperor a *sanad* [28] conferring on him the governorship of Bengal." [29] It was apparently Holwell's intention to prove that the House of 'Alivardi, which the English ousted from power, had no real claim on the throne of Bengal. In his view, the Maratha invasion was the result of an entreaty made in the Emperor's name to send " an army of sufficient force to exact the amount of the *Chout* " from Bengal, and also to take the heads of 'Alivardi and his brother. The Rājā of Sātārā [30] now had a " justifiable plea to attack the Mogul's dominions with his own consent; therefore without loss of time, he ordered an army of 80,000 horse to take the field and march into Bengal, under the command of Bhaskar Pandit." But however much Holwell disliked 'Alivardi, he was not blind to the Nawāb's " intrepid qualities " and the " amazing courage " with which he tried to check the invaders.[31]

Another account is that of Luke Scrafton, who was a friend of Robert Clive.[32] Scrafton's view is that the Marathas were en-

25. *Ibid.*, pp. 109-110.
26. A robe of honor, presented by a king or emperor.
27. Sarkar, *Bengal Nawābs*, p. 24.
28. A letter of certification.
29. *Ibid.*, p. 91.
30. I. e., Sāhu Rājā.
31. Holwell, *Interesting Historical Events*, pp. 109, 114.
32. Robert Clive (1725-1774) came to Madras in 1744, as a writer of the East India Company, returned to England in 1753 and again came to India in 1755; went to Bengal from Madras after the " Black Hole " of Calcutta and recovered Calcutta from Sirāj-ud-daulah's troops; defeated the Nawāb in the battle of Plassey and became virtual ruler of Bengal; raised Mir Jāfar to the position

couraged to attack Bengal by the Emperor Muhammad Shāh: "The Emperor, brought to the last state of imbecility by the invasions of Nadir Shah,[33] and unable either to resist or comply, proposed to them among other expedients, to send a force against Allyvherde Caun to receive the revenues of the last two years; send his and his brother's heads to court; and reinstate the family of Shujah [Khān]." [34]

Scrafton avoided recounting the skirmishes and other military operations involved in the Maratha raids, though he does give a summary of the raids up to the treaty of 1751, which, however, he wrongly puts one year earlier.[35]

OTHER NOTICES OF THE TEXT

The present work is not the first notice which has been taken of the *Mahārāshṭa Purāṇa*. As has been earlier noted, the text was published in the *Sāhitya pariṣad patrikā* in B. S. 1307 (A. D. 1907-1908), with introduction and notes by Byomakesh Mustafi. At that time the text was received with a good deal of interest, though there were some errors of fact in the introduction and notes. In 1917, Professor J. N. Das Gupta published an interpretive article on the text and the period of history with which it deals in *The Calcutta Review*.[36] In 1924, Professor J. N. Samaddar of Patna University sent a paper on the *Mahārāshṭa Purāṇa* to the annual meeting of the Indian Historical Records Commission,[37] and in that same year published a somewhat abridged English translation of the text with notes and brief introduction.[38] A second English translation of the

of the Nawāb; Governor of the East India Company's territories in Bengal 1757-60; left for England in 1760; second governorship of Bengal, 1765-67.

33. King of Persia who in 1739 invaded India at the head of a great army and sacked Delhi.
34. Luke Scrafton, *Reflections on the Government of Indostan* (London: printed by W. Richardson, 1763).
35. *Ibid.*, p. 40.
36. Das Gupta, "An Eighteenth Century Bengali Manuscript," *op. cit.*
37. See *Proceedings of the Indian Historical Records Commission* for 1924 (Delhi, Manager of Publications).
38. "The Maratha Invasion of Bengal in 1743, as told in the Maharashtra Purana," *Bengal Past and Present* (Journal of the Calcutta Historical Society), XXVII, January-March 1924.

text was published in 1930 by Dr. T. C. Dasgupta.[39] The historical material in the text has also been utilized by Professor Kalikinkar Datta in his *Alivardi and His Times*,[40] and by Dr. Jadunath Sarkar in the *History of Bengal*,[41] in his *Fall of the Mughal Empire*, Vol. I, and in a series of historical articles published in the journal *Prabāsī*.[42]

CHARACTERISTICS OF THE TEXT

The *Mahārāshṭa Purāṇa* is an unusual text for several reasons. First of all, despite its Puranic lip-service, it is basically a text of pure secular history, and, except for the chronicles of the Muslim courts, we are not usually inclined to associate Bengal with historical writing. One unfamiliar with the conventions of medieval Bengali literature may be amused at the part the gods and goddesses play in shaping the destinies of men, at divine capriciousness, at divinities swayed by human passions and activities. But despite its Puranic veneer, the main outline of the text rings amazingly true in such worldly details as topography. To say that " in every detail [the text] tallies with existing records " and that the text is reliable because of its " unvarnished language " and " want of emotion " might be a slight exaggeration. Though Gaṅgārām's style is simple and free from hyperbole, he is writing a poem; and one cannot write a poem without a touch of color or emotion. Yet the text is as valuable for its historical detail as it is for the story which it tells.

For the story is a good one, and it is well told. The writer has a sense of dry humor which shows through the anguish of the situation which he describes. And there are frequent passages of low-keyed description which come movingly to life. Sometimes, it is true, the accounts of eighteenth-century warfare seem to us, accustomed to more massive slaughter, like comic opera. Spokesmen from rival armies on the brink of battle indulge in almost irrelevant wars of words; the march of an army harassed and being cut to pieces by a swiftly riding foe is as colorful as a wedding

39. In *Journal of the Department of Letters* (University of Calcutta), XX, 1930.
40. University of Calcutta, 1939.
41. Volume II; Dacca University, 1948, pp. 455 ff.
42. *Prābasī*, B.S. 1337-1338 (A.D. 1931-1932), XXX, XXXI.

procession; cannons blow up in peoples' faces at awkward times. Yet, behind it all there is the backdrop of a Bengal terrorstricken, caught in the path of onslaught; and this is anything but comic opera. It is blood and the brutal savageness of a conquering army. The scenes of village people fleeing the rape and looting, the fire of their burning villages lighting the night sky, are real and terrifying. For the people of Bengal, it was a horror remembered to this day, even in nursery rhyme:

> The baby sleeps, and all the countryside's at rest,
> but the *bargis* have invaded our country.
> The *bulbuli* birds have eaten all the rice;
> how can we pay the rent?
> (There is no more rice, no more *pān* leaves.
> How shall we pay the tax?)

The text of the *Mahārāshṭa Purāṇa* shows us the reason for the bitterness which lies beneath.

THE EFFECTS OF THE MARATHA RAIDS

The Maratha raids had their effect, although Bengal was not "long conquered by Rāghuji."[43] The Marathas actually secured only the province of Orissa, which they held until the beginning of the nineteenth century. Fear of the raids, indeed, lessened trade in West Bengal and caused migration; but whether there was sufficient movement of refugees to northern and eastern Bengal to change radically the balance of the population in the Province may be questioned.[44] One immediate and lasting result of the Maratha incursions, however, was the rapid growth of the city of Calcutta. People who had been living on the western bank of the Hughli found it safer to cross the river and live under the protection of the East India Company. Although the Marathas never attacked Calcutta, the threat was there; there still remains a trace of the "Maratha Ditch," dug to protect the city. It was originally planned to be a semicircular canal, which was to start from the Hughli

43. G. S. Sardesai, *Main Currents of Maratha History* (2nd. ed.; Bombay: Phoenix Publications, 1949), p. 114.
44. Kalikinkar Datta, *Alivardi and His Times*, p. 217.

River north of the city, and join the river again in the south, in the area known as Govindapur. Except for a small section, the ditch was later filled in by order of Lord Wellesley. In Orissa, there remain some signs of Maratha rule, but in Bengal the vanishing Maratha Ditch, the text of the *Mahārāshṭa Purāṇa*, and the terrible memory preserved in local ballads and rhymes are the only remaining traces of the coming of the *bargis*.

THE MAHĀRĀSHṬA PURĀṆA

translation — transliteration

The people of the earth were filled with sin, and there was no worship of Rādhā and Kṛṣṇa.[1] Day and night the people took their pleasure with the wives of others. No one knew what might happen at any time. Day and night were spent in amorous sport, and in abusing others and doing injury to them. There was no thought of anything else. So great was this burden of sin upon the earth that Earth was unable to bear it. So Earth went to Brahmā [2] and said to him:

—Because of sin, Lord, the earth has become a great burden. My pain is so great that I can no longer bear it.

When he heard this, Brahmā said:

—Do not be anxious, but put your mind at rest.

And, taking Earth, Brahmā went to the place of Śiva [3] and said to Śiva in flattering words:

—Lord, you are the Creator. You are the Destroyer. You are Nārāyaṇa.[4] You are the movable and the immovable; you are the pure.[5] You are the mother and father and friend. The circle of the earth,[6] O Lord, is your creation.

1. The divine conceived as heavenly lovers, worshipped by the Vaiṣṇavas. Kṛṣṇa is also considered as an incarnation of Viṣṇu, also known as "Nārāyaṇa," "Hari," and by other names.
2. A Hindu god; the creator of the Universe.
3. An important god of the Hindu pantheon. Śiva is the consort of Durgā; one of his many names is Trilocana (Three-eyed-one), because of a third eye on his forehead. Śiva is Hara, the Destroyer.
4. According to Hindu mythology, Nārāyaṇa is variously the creative principle floating on the primeval cosmic waters, the son of the original Man (see *Mānavadharma-śāstra* I: 10), identified with Brahmā (*ibid.*, I: 11), later identified with Viṣṇu, Kṛṣṇa, etc.
5. A traditional description of the ultimate principle; "*nirañjana*" means pure, spotless.
6. Or "the orb of the earth"—*e mahi maṇḍala.*

śrīśrīkṛṣṇa

rādhākṛṣṇa nāhi bhaje pāpamati haiñā /
rātradina kṛḍa kare parastrī laiñā //
śrīṅgāra kautuke jiba thāke sarbbakṣana / 1
hena nāhi jāne sei ki habe kakhana //
parahiṅsā paranindā kare rātridine /
ei sakala kathā bine anya nāhi mane //
eta jadi pāpa haila pṛthibi upare /
pāpera kārane pṛthi bhāra bhāra sahite nāre // 2
tabe pṛthi cali gelā braḥmāra gocara /
kahite lāgīlā pṛthī braḥmā barābara //
pāpera kārane prabhu pṛthī haila bhāri /
kata byāma pāba āmī bhāra sahīte nāri //
eteka suniñā brāḥmā boliche bacana /
byāku nā haiya tumi dharyya kara mana // 3
pṛthī saṅge kari braḥmā gelā śība sttāne /
kahite lāgilā braḥmā sttati bacane //
tumi karttā tumi harttā tumi nārāyana /
sthābara jaṅgama tumi nirañjana //
tumi mātā tumi pītā tumī bandhujana /
e mahi maṇḍala prabhu tomāra śrijana //

1. /kṣ/ in Bengali has the same phonetic value as /kh/.
2. The repetition of /bhāra/ may be a scribal error; the first one occurs at the end of a line in the MS.
3. Mustaphi has /byākula nā/, which is possible only if the scribe has erred. Either interpretation makes sense.

In these words of praise spoke Brahmā, and Śiva[7] was pleased, and, smiling, replied to him:
—Tell me, why do you make such entreaty?

And Brahmā smiled, and said to Trilocana:
—It has happened that Earth can no longer bear her burden because of the peoples' sin. The people are evil, and do evil deeds. Strike down these evil people, Lord. Rid Earth of her burden.

When he heard this, Hara said:
—I shall send an agent and strike down the sinful people.

And when Śiva had said this to Brahmā, Brahmā took Earth and went to his own place. There he bade farewell to Earth, and Earth returned home, meditating upon these things. And when Brahmā had gone, Śiva remained sunk in meditation.

Some time later, Śiva remembered these things and called Nandī[8] and said to him:
—Go now to the city in the south.[9] There is a king on earth, Sāhurājā[10] by name. Go to him, and enter into his body. Much sin and evil have come upon the earth. Let him send his agents,

7. *Saṅkara* (*śaṅkara*), the Auspicious, the Beneficent.
8. The principal attendant of Śiva. Śiva rides a white bull, the image of which is seen outside his shrine. This bull is called Nandī.
9. The reference is to Sātārā, about 50 miles south of Poona in Mahārāshṭra, where the Maratha king ordinarily resided. Later on, the importance of Sātārā declined, and from 1750 Poona became the center of Maratha power.
10. I. e., Śāhurājā. In the MS, the writer or the scribe in most cases uses the dental sibilant symbol for all three sibilants (Introduction, p. xii, n. 8). Exceptions to this are such cases as the name of Śiva, in which he uses the proper symbol for the palatal sibilant; a likely reason for this inconsistency is that the writer or scribe had seen the name of Śiva written, while the name of Śāhurājā was most likely recorded from the spoken word.

Śāhurājā was the grandson of Śivaji, founder of the Maratha power; he had been prisoner in the Mughal camp while young and was freed after Aurangzeb's death (1707); he died in 1749. During his reign, Maratha power expanded to the north.

eteka binaya jadi kailā braḥmābara /
hāsiñā tāhāre tabe balilā saṅkara //
eteka minati kara kīsera kāraṇa /
bola dekhi suni āmi tāhāra bibarana //
tabe braḥmā kahilen hāsi trilocane / 1
pṛthī bhāra sahite nāre pāpera kāraṇe //
pāpamati haila jiba kare durācāra /
pāpīṣṭa māriā prabhu dura kara bhāra //
kahite lāgilā hara eteka suniñā /
pāpīṣṭa mārichi āmī duta pāṭhāiñā // 2
eteka balilā jadi braḥmāra gocara /
pṛthī saṅge braḥmā tabe gelā āpana ghara //
tabe braḥmā bidāe karilā pṛthīre /
bhābite$_2$ pṛthī āilā yāpana ghare // 3
braḥmāke bidāe diyā śība railā dhyāne /
kathokṣana pare sei kathā paila mane //
nandīke ḍākīyā siba baliche bacana / 4
dakṣina sahare tumi jāha tatakṣana //
sāhurājā nāme eka āche pṛthibite /
adhiṣṭhāna haya jāiā tāhāra dehete //
biparita pāpa haila pṛthībi upare /
duta pāṭhāiñā jena (pāpe loka māre) //

1. Mustaphi has /balilen/ for MS /kahilen/.
2. Mustaphi omits /āmī/.
3. The subscript is a scribal convention indicating that the form is to be repeated; thus /bhābite bhābite/, while thinking.
4. Scribal inconsistency typical of the text is obvious here; two lines above the scribe has written /śība/.

that the sinners and evildoers be punished.[11]

When he had heard this, Nandī went swiftly to Sāhurājā. Then Sāhurājā said to Raghurājā: [12]

—The *cauth* of Bengal has not been paid to me for a long time. Send a messenger to the Bādsā [13] and ask him why he has not sent me the *cauth* of Bengal. Write a letter to the Bādsā, that a messenger might take it to him quickly.

So Raghurājā wrote a letter of few words, and a messenger took the letter and tied it in his turban. Next morning he went swiftly, and bore the letter to the Emperor at Delhi. The Emperor then gave this order to his *ujīr*: [14]

—Read the letter aloud to me.

The *ujīr* read the letter, and the Bādsā listened.

—Sāhurājā writes in regard to the *cauth* of Bengal.

Then the Bādsā gave this order to his *ujīr*:

—Write this to Sāhurājā. "He who was a servant has killed the governor; he has become very powerful, and does not pay me the tax.[15] I have no army. I have no one who can bring him here. He enjoys his kingdom in Bengal in great happiness and has not paid me the tax for two years. He is very powerful

11. Literally, killed. The reference is to the invasions of Bengal, viewed as retribution for evil deeds.

12. I. e., Rāghuji Bhonsle, Maratha ruler of Nagpur.

13. *Bādsā*, i. e., Badshāh, Emperor. The reference is to the Emperor Muhammad Shāh of Delhi (1719-1748).

14. *Ujīr*, i. e., wazir, principal minister. Muhammad Shāh's wazir was Qamr-ud-din, entitled Itīmād-ud-daulah II, who held office from 1724 to 1748. He is described in *Siyār-ul-Mutākherīn* (Vol. III, pp. 280-281) as "slothful, inattentive, indolent and eternally immersed in all kinds of pleasures" but so "inoffensive and such an enemy to oppression, that the people of the capital remember him with regret even to this very day . . . a magnificent friend and a bountiful patron, but a weak vazier wanting firmness and activity."

15. *Lālabandi*, or *nālbandi*, literally, horseshoe money (*nāl*, horseshoe). Horace H. Wilson, *Glossary of Judicial and Revenue Terms* (Calcutta, 1940), says: "Under the Mohammedan government, a contribution exacted from petty

. . . pāpe loka māre //
eteka śuniñā nandi gelā sigragati / 1
upanita hailā giyā sāhurājā prati //
sāhurājā bole tabe raghūrājāra tare / 2
aneka dina haila bāṅgālāra cauta nā dee more //
duta pāṭhāiyā dea bādsāra sthāne /
bāṅgālāra cauthāi nā dee kīsera kārane //
eka khāni patra likha bādāsā prati /
duta jene tāhā laiyā jāe sigragati //
raghurājā patra likhe ākhara pāc sāte /
patra laiñā duta tabe badhilen māthe //
rajani prabhāte duta jāe sigragati /
patra āsi dilen jekhāne dillipati // 3
ujirake yājñā tabe dilā dillisvare /
sīgragati patra paḍi sunāya āmāre // 4
ujira paṛen patra bādasā sunenâ /
sāhurājā likhe bāṅgālāra cauthera kāraṇâ //
bādasā tabe ājñā dilā ujirere /
patra likhaha tumi sāhurājāre //
cākara haiā mārileka subāre / 5
jabara haila lālabandi nā deyā māre // 6
loka laskara tabe nāi āmāra sthāne /
hena konajana nāhi tāre giyā āne //
bāṅgālā muluka sei bhuñje parama sukhe /
dui batsara haila lālabandi nā dee meke // 7

1. The second word in the line is unclear in the MS.
2. The last two words in the line unclear; the first folio ends with this line.
3. The last word unclear; we have followed Mustaphi.
4. /sunāya/ is unclear in MS; the form is questionable.
5. Mustaphi has /mārile/, and the MS is blurred at this point.
6. Or /deya āmāre/; in the MS it is written as a compound, /deyāmāre/.
7. /meke/ is a scribal error or dialect form of /moke/, to me.

in Bengal. Therefore you should send men there to take the *cauth*."

Such was the letter which the *ujīr* wrote. The messenger took it, bowed his head in salutation, and left. He went swiftly to Setārā [Sātārā]. The king had convened his court, and was sitting in the throne room; it was then that the messenger arrived with the letter. He gave it to the king and stood to one side with folded hands. The king then ordered his *dewān*[16] to read the letter and the *dewān* read it aloud:

—"The *subā*[17] of Bengal is strong. Two years have passed since they last paid the revenue.[18] The Bādsā directs that an army be sent to take the *cauth* by force."

When he heard this, the king said:

—Whom then shall I send to Bengal?

Raghurājā was seated nearby, and he said, smiling:

—Order me to go to Bengal. I shall take the *cauth* by force.

The king so ordered him. Then Raghurājā sent for his *dewān* Bhāskara, and ordered him:

—Bring the *cauth* to me without delay!

When he had received this order from the Rājā, Bhāskara

princes or the peasantry, on the plea of keeping up the cavalry of the State, or as the price of preventing the horsemen from devastating the country, but which was converted into a small permanent tribute: among the Marathas, the equipment of cavalry for the field, or an advance to a troop when enlisted or sent on service."

16. *Dewān* or *diwān*—See Wilson, *Glossary*:
"A royal court, a council of State, a tribunal of revenue or justice. A minister, a chief officer of states . . . under the Maratha government the *Diwān* was the chief minister after the *Pradhan*. . . ."

17. "*Subā*" means province; among the Marathas the term was sometimes applied to smaller divisions. See Wilson, *Glossary*. "*Subā*" is also occasionally used to mean "*Subādār*" (Governor).

18. "*Khājānā*" is rent or revenue.

jabara haiñā sei āche bāṅgālāte /
cauthera kārane loka pāṭhāya tathāte //
eteka bacana patre likhīlā ujira /
patra pāiñā duta tabe noñāilā sira //
tabe duta bidāe hailā turite /
sigragati yāsi pahacilā setārāte //
sabhā kariñā rājā baisā āche dyāne / 1
henakāle patra duta āne seikhāne //
patra āsi dilā duta rājāra gocara /
ḍāṛāilā eka bhite kari joṛakara //
ājñā dilā deo(w)ānake patra paṛibāre /
patra paṛiyā deo(w)āna sunāna rājāre //
jabara haila sūbā bāṅgālā sahare /
dui batsara haila khājānā nā dee tāre //
ājñā dilā bādasā phoja pāṭhāiñā /
cauthāi neena jena jabara kariñā //
eteka sūniñā rājā lāgilā kahite /
konajanāke pāṭhāba muluka bāṅgālāte //
raghurājā nikaṭe āchilā basiā /
kahite lāgilā tini hāsiyā$_2$ //
ājñā kara bāṅgālā muluke āmi jāi /
jabara kariyā tathā āniba cauthāi //
tabe tāre ājñā dilen rājana /
tini pāṭhāilen deo(w)āna bhāskarana //
raghu tabe ājñā dilā bhāskare /
tatkāna kariyā cauthāi āni dibā more // 2
rājāra ādesa pāiyā bhāskara . . .

1. MS unclear on last word.
2. Mustaphi has /tatpara/ for the first word in the line; the MS, however, is clear.

marched quickly with army and equipment. And with kettle-drums [19] beating and with music the army marched forth under streaming banners. They left Setārā and came to Bijāpur, and there they camped for one night. That night in the camp there was music and dancing and much festivity, and the next day the army departed. By many villages and forests they marched. They arrived at Nāgpur. They left there, and shortly arrived at Pañckoṭ [Pachet].[20] At that place Bhāskara called a messenger and said to him:

—Go and find out where the Nabāb [21] is.

So the messenger went quickly and inquired where the Nabāb was. When he had gained this information he hastened back [to Bhāskara] and said:

—The Nabāb is in Bardhamān [Burdwan] city, [camped] on the bank of the Rāni's tank.[22]

Learning this from his messenger, Bhāskara went forth with his army in the still of night. The army marched silently, and no one knew of their presence. It was the nineteenth of Baiśākh [23] when the Bargis came, with joy in their hearts. Keeping Birbhūm to their left and passing near Gowālā-bhum, they came to Bardhamān and surrounded the city. The Bargis

19. The term is "*ḍaṅkā nāgārā.*" *Ḍaṅkā* is a big drum. *Nāgārā* is a pair of kettledrums, 2½ to 3 feet in diameter. See Bibliography, under "Sachs" and "Sambamoorthy."

20. Pachet (Panchet) hill in Manbhum district, W. Bengal, about 100 miles west of Burdwan. At the foot of the hill is the fort, residence of the *Rājā* of Panchet. For references to Panchet by Yusuf 'Ali and G͟hulām Husain Salīm, see Appendix II, p. 71.

21. I. e., Nawāb. The Nawāb referred to throughout the text, though never by name, is 'Alivardi Khān. He was formerly Governor of Bihar; he rebelled against his master Sarfarāz Khān and seized power by defeating him in battle. He ruled from 1740 to 1756.

22. Actually, the Marathas came in contact with the Nawāb's army in the outskirts of the city of Burdwan.

23. "Baiśākh" is April-May, the first month of the Indian calendar year. The 19th of the month would be about the 4th of May.

(rājāra ādesa pāiyā bhāskara) calila dhāiyā 1
sanya saṅge kariyā sājana /
ḍaṅkā nāgārā kata nīsāna cale sata$_2$
sanya madhe bājiche bājana //
setārā chāḍiyā jabe bijāpūra āilā tabe 2
eka rātri railā seikhāne /
rāgaraṅga haila jata nāṭu(w)ā nācila kata
kaṭaka calila paradine //
grāma upabana kata laskara eḍāe jata
nāgapūra āsi upanita /
sekhāna chāḍiyā jabe laskara yāila tabe
pañcakoṭe āsilā turita //
ḍāka diyā dutake bhāskara kahila tāke
nabāba āche konakhāne /
ājñā dilā senāpati duta cale sigragati
nabāba yāche jeikhāne //
duta sambāda laiyā sigra calila dhāiyā
āsiyā kahila tārasthāne //
baddamāna sahare rānira dighira pare
nabāba āche seikhāne //
dutamukhe suni kathā bhāskara calila tathā
laskara laiyā nisāte / 3
laskara nisabde jāe kehu nāhi jāne tāe
āilā baisākha uniśāte //
baisāgera unisā jāe baragi āila tāe
mahā yānandita haiyā mane /
birabhui bāme thuiyā goālābhuiera kācha haiyā
āsiyā gherila baddamāne //

1. The first section in *tripadi* meter begins here.
2. Mustaphi has /setārā chāṛiyā tabe/.
3. The last word of the line is not clear in the MS.

came and surrounded the city on all four sides, and the sentries did not know of it at all. In the second watch of the night a sentry came and reported to Rājārām,[24] and as the night became morning Rājārām went to the place where the Nabāb was and said:

—I did not know—an army has come suddenly and has surrounded our troops.

The Nabāb listened to what Rājārām said, and then gave his answer:

—Send spies and find the truth of this matter. Whence came this army?

When he heard that, [Rājārām] sent spies to find out about the army. Having disguised themselves, they moved among the troops, and brought back this message to the Nabāb:

—There are twenty-four *jamādārs*,[25] and Bhāskara is their leader. With them are forty thousand troops. They are Bargis, come from Setārā fort to take the *cauth* by the command of Sāhurājā.

When he heard this, the Nabāb called together his *jamādārs* in council and said to them:

24. Rājārām was Rājārām Singh, chief of 'Alivardi's espionage department. See Datta, *'Alivardi and His Times*, p. 164.

25. "*Jamādār*"—a petty officer.

tabe baragīra laskare catudige yāsi ghire
harakārā kehu nāhi jāne /
dui prahar rāite harakārā āila tāthe
āsī kaila rājārāma sthāne //
rajani prabhāta haila rājārāma harakārā āila
āsiyā kahila nabābere /
ihā yāmi nā jānila ācambite sanya āila
āsiyā gherila laskare //
rājārāme eta kae nabāba sūniyā rae
tadapare dilen uttara /
harakārā pāṭhāiyā hakīkata āna jāyā
kauthā haite yāila laskara // 1
eteka sunila jabe harakārā pāṭhāila tabe
phojera nirnnae jānibāre / 2
sājiñā harakārā laskare phire tārā
āsiyā kahila nabābere //
cambis jamādāra bhāskara saradāra
callisa hājāra phoja laiñā /
setārā gaḍa haite baragī āila cautha nite
sāhurājār hukuma pāiñā //
eteka kathā sūniyā jamādāra āne ḍākiyā
kahite lāgilā nabāba /

1. The first two words are unclear in the MS.
2. The second word is unclear; we have followed Mustaphi.

—The Bargis have come from Setārā to take the *cauth*. What is your answer to that? When Śujā Khān was alive, revenue used to be sent to the Emperor of Delhi to pay the *cauth*.[26]

Mustaphā Khān [27] said:

—Do now what is in your mind.

[Mustaphā Khān] then said to the *ukīl*: [28]

—Why has he come with his army prepared for battle? Go and ask him that.

So the *ukīl* went and spoke to Bhāskara, and when Bhāskara had heard him out he said:

—Sāhurājā has sent me here to take the *cauth*. That is why I have come. Go and tell the Nabāb to give the *cauth* to me. Go quickly.

But when he had heard this, the *ukīl* replied:

—You say things which are not proper—that Bargis should come to Bengal at any time to take the *cauth* is a great wrong.[29]

Then Bhāskara said to him:

—Whose is the wrong? Have you considered this—by whose command has [the Nabāb] usurped this province? By what justice does he refuse to pay tribute to the emperor?

26. And the Marathas used to collect it from there. Śujā Khān was former Nawāb of Bengal (1727-1739), father of Sarfarāz Khān.

27. Ghulām Mustaphā Khān was one of the chief advisors and one of the greatest of the Afghan generals of 'Alivardi Khān, "exalted above all the other captains by reason of his firm loyalty and devotion" (Yusuf 'Ali in *Bengal Nawābs*, p. 95). Mustaphā Khān helped 'Alivardi in the assassination of Bhāskara. Later on, he left 'Alivardi's service and became a rebel.

28. I. e., "*vākīl*," a representative of the crown; a court pleader or counsel.

29. The *vākīl* argues that the *cauth* should be collected from the Emperor at Delhi and not directly from Bengal.

setārā gaḍa haite baragi āila cautha nite
ihā ki bolaha jabāba //
bādasāi khājānā jāita sekhāne cauthāi pāita
śujā khā āchila jakhana /
mustaphā khā eta kae jāhā tomāra citte lae
tāhā tumi karaha ekhana //
ukīlake kahila sanya sāijā kena āila
ei kathā bala jāiyā tāre /
ukila kahen kathā bhāskara śunen tathā
tabeta kahila tārapare //
sāhurājā pāṭhāe more cauthāi nibāra tare
tekārane āilām āmi /
jāiyā bola nabābere cautha jena dee more
sigragati cali jāha tumi //
eteka sūniyā jabe ukīla kahila tare
anyāe kathā kene bola /
konakāle bāṅgālāte baragī yāise cautha nite
eita yanyāya baḍa haila //
bhāskara bulila tāre kebā yanyāe kare
manete kaile bhābanā /
kāhāra hukuma pāiyā mūluka nilā māriyā
bādasāi khājānā bheja nā //

To this [the *ukīl*] replied:
—You do not know how to collect the *cauth.* You should have sent an agent to him; if the agent had spoken to the Nabāb, he would have paid the *cauth* later. Take your army and depart. Say to the Emperor that if he sends a *sanad,*[30] the *khājānā* will be sent. You will receive the *cauth* [in Delhi].

But Bhāskara said:
—The Bādsā has ordered me to take the *cauth.*[31] If you do not give it to me I shall make war upon you, and I shall destroy this kingdom!

When he heard this, the *ukīl* replied:
—Sir, you are trying to frighten him in vain. Your army is encamped on all sides. Yet what will they be able to do [against us]? If there were thousands of men like you, the Nabāb would have no fear. Everyone in all the earth[32] knows that there are no soldiers like those of the Nabāb.

Thus Bhāskara heard the reply of the [Nabāb's] *ukīl* and said to him:
—If he does not pay the *cauth* to me, I shall make war. Go and tell him this.

30. "*sanad*"—a charter or grant from royal authority.

31. Yusuf 'Ali (in *Bengal Nawābs,* p. 97) says:

"At that time envoys from both sides opened negotiations; and Bhāskara, seeing that without hard fighting it would be difficult for him to gain his object, sent a message that he would return to his own country if 'Alivardi paid him ten lakhs of rupees."

32. The text reads "*caukhuta muluke,*" literally, four-cornered kingdom.

suniyā uttara dilā cautha nite nā jānilā
ukila pāṭhāitā tāra kāche /
ukila jāiyā pare kahita nabāba tare
cauthāi diten tinī pāche //
āpana kaṭaka laiyā puna jāya phiriyā
kaha tabe bādasāra sthāne /
sanuda jadi dee khājānā tabe jae
cauthāi pābe seikhāne //
bhāskara tabe kae bādasāra hukuma hae
cautha nibāra kāraṇa /
cauthāi nā dibe jabe rāyya naṣṭa habe tabe
tāra sane kariba āmi rana //
eteka bacana suni ukila kahena bāni
bhae tumi ki dekhāya tāre / 1
tomāra jateka senā catudige dila thānā
tārā saba kī karite pāre //
tumi jemana eka janā emana āise sahaśra janā
taba tāra bhurūkṣepa nāi /
caukhuṭā muluke sabhāi jānae tāke
nabābera samāna ke āche sipāi //
ukila bulilā jabe bhāskara janilā tabe
kahite lāgilā tārapare /
cauthāi nā dibe jabe juddha kariba tabe
ei kathā bola jāiyā tāre //

1. Mustaphi reads /bhadra/ for /bhae/, fear, but the MS is clear at this point. Mustaphi also has /kise/ for /ki/ in this line.

So the *ukīl* returned and said to the Nabāb:
—He will make war.

When the Nabāb heard this he called his *jamādārs* and told them:
—He demands the *cauth* again and again.

The *sārdārs* who had assembled then replied:
—Instead, give the money to the soldiers. We are many men.[33] We shall kill the Bargis. They shall not enter our country. We shall kill them all, and they shall not enter our land. What can Bhāskara do against us?

When he heard these words the Nabāb was greatly pleased, and he said to them:
—Good! You have spoken well.

Then he distributed *pan*[34] to all who were in the court, from a *pan*-box which was lying nearby, and bade farewell to them all.[35]

Then the commander Bhāskara summoned all his *jamādārs* and said to them:
—Some of you set up outposts on all sides. Some go forth and plunder.

Thus the commander spoke. The *jamādārs* dressed for battle

33. "*Sārdār*"—army officer, chief.
There were not really many men. For Yusuf 'Ali's references to this, see Appendix II, p. 71.

34. Betel-leaf, dressed with lime, nuts, and sometimes tobacco and other ingredients. From a superior authority it was a sign of favor. *Pān* was often distributed before the dispersal of formal assembly; the practice was observed even in British days.

35. Either Yusuf 'Ali or Gaṅgārām is a little confused about the sequence of events here. Yusuf 'Ali (pp. 97-98) has this decision to stand fast first taken by 'Alivardi and then supported by Mustaphā Khān, over the advice to pay the demand given by Jānaki Rām and others of the high officers. Yusuf 'Ali also has the whole incident take place after the pitched battle on the march from Burdwan to Kaṭwā, after another surrender ultimatim from Bhāskara, which Gaṅgārām does not mention.

ukila āsiñā pare kahila nabāba tare
rana karite seha cāhe /
eteka suniñā jabe nabāba janila tabe 1
ḍāka diyā jamādāre kahe //
jata jamādāra chila tāre nabāba kahila
cauthāi cāhe bāre$_2$ /
jateka saradāra chila tārā saba kahila
sei ṭākā deha sipāere //
āmarā jata loke māriba baragike
dese jena yā āiste nāi pāre / 2
baragi saba māriba dese āiste nā diba 3
kī karite pāre bhāskare // 4
suniñā eteka bāni santuṣṭa hailā tini 5
kahite lāgilā bhāla$_2$ /
pānabāṭā kāche chila pāna tuilā sabhāre dila
bidāe haiyā sabhe āila //
ethā bhāskara saradāre ḍāka dee jamādāre
kahite lāgilā ta sabhāre /
tomarā kata janā catudige deya thānā
kata janā jāya luṭībāre //
saradāre kahe eta sāje jamādāra kata
(catudige jāe luṭībāra /)

1. Probably a scribal error for /jānila/.
2. Mustaphi's text has no /yā/; there is, in all probability, an error, and the text should read /yāiste/.
3. The last word in the line is unclear in the MS.
4. The line is unclear in MS.
5. Mustaphi's text has /suniyā/, but the MS is clear at this point.

and set forth in all directions to plunder. Many men there were who prepared themselves for battle; hear now of them. I shall list their names one by one.

Dhāmadharmā went, and Hirāman Kāsi, and Gaṅgāji Āmaṛa, and Simanta Josi; Bālāji went forth, and Sevāji Kohaṛā, and Sambhūji, and Kesaji Āmoṛa; Kesari Siṅha and Mahana Siṅha, two Cāmārs, also went. With these men went five companies of horse.[36] These ten went to loot the villages, while fourteen others remained around the camp of the Nabāb—Bālārāo, Seśrāo, Sis-paṇḍit, Semanta Sehaṛā, Hirāman Maṇḍita,[37] Mohana Rāe, Pita Rāe, Siso-paṇḍit, and with these many evil Bargis; there were also Nirāji, Sāmāji, and Phiraṅga Rāe,[38] with whom the Bargis ran wildly to loot and plunder; and there were . . . .,[39] and Sunātana Khān, and Bhāskara. These fourteen surrounded the army [of the Nabāb].

One day passed, and two—and for seven days the Bargis besieged [the camps] and cut off the food supply. The grocers and merchants could not go outside, for the Bargis plundered, cut down and killed everyone they found. No one dared to go

36. The term "*hār*," which is here translated as "company," is an obscure one; another possible translation, though perhaps a less likely one, is *hājār* or thousand. The term "*hār*" appears more than once in the text.

37. A scribal error for "*paṇḍita*"?

38. "*Phiraṅga*" is a term used to indicate a European or one of European and Indian parentage. Whether "*phiraṅga rāe*" is here meant to refer to an individual who was himself a European or whether it indicates a leader of Europeans is open to question. There were mercenary troops, Europeans and otherwise, in many Indian armies of the time.

39. Two words in the MS here cannot be deciphered.

catudige jāe luṭībāra
sājila jata jana suna bhāra bibarana 1
eke$_2$ nāma bali tāra // 2

dhāmadharamā jāe āra hirāmana kāsi /
gaṅgāji āmaḍā jāe yāra simanta josi //
bālāji jāe āra sebāji koharā /
sambhuji jāe āra kesaji āmoṛa //
kesari siṅha mahana siṅha e dui cāmāra /
jāra saṅge jāe ghoḍa pāca hāra //
ei dasa janā jāe grāma luṭite / 3
āra cauda janā thāke nabābera cāira bhite //
bālārāo seśa rāo āra sisapaṇḍita /
semanta sehaṛā āra hirāmana maṇḍita // 4
mohana rāe pita rāe āra siso paṇḍita /
jāra saṅge āche baragi mahābiparita //
nirāji sāmāji āra phiraṅga rāe / 5
lūṭite jāhāra saṅge baragi drita dhāe //
ā . . . sunantāna khā āra bhāskara / 6
ei cauda janāte gherila laskara //
ekadina duidina kari sāta di haila /
catudige baragīte rasada bandha kaila //
mudibānīñā jata bārāite nāre /
luṭe kāṭe mārechmute (pāe jāre) //

1. Mustaphi reads /śuna/.
2. The *tripadi* section ends here.
3. The line is unclear in MS.
4. The last words in the line are illegible; the lower right corner of the folio is badly faded.
5. The first word in the line is faded.
6. One word in the lower right corner of the MS had been obliterated. The second word in the line begins the next folio.

out, for fear of the Bargis, nor could they get their supply of provisions. For rice, pulses, peas, *musri*,[40] *khesāri*,[41] oil, *ghi*,[42] *āṭā*,[43] sugar, and salt, and for vegetables also the price was one rupee a seer;[44] even then no one could buy them. Poor people died of starvation. And *gājā*,[45] *bhāṅg*,[46] and tobacco could not be bought at any price. No vegetables could be had; the people were frightened. They boiled and ate the roots of young plantain trees. All the people in the army, both great and small, cooked and lived on boiled plantain roots. The hardship was very great. The Nabāb himself ate these roots. What shall I say of others? And the army remained like this for fourteen days.[47]

Then the Nabāb marched out with all his army.[48] First came the mounted standard-bearers with streaming banners, drums and kettledrums booming, and after this attendants playing lively music and then the troopers,[49] [their horses] prancing before the Nabāb. The great army spread to all the four horizons, and there was no numbering of them. But then the Bargis

40. Lentils.
41. A variety of pulse.
42. Clarified butter.
43. Wheat or wheatflour.
44. In modern Bengal, a seer is slightly more than two pounds Troy weight.
45. Indian hemp.
46. A form of drug, usually taken in liquid mixture.
47. Texts vary on the description of the siege and on the length of time which it lasted. Yusuf 'Ali has the Nawāb surrounded in a field after marching forth immediately to engage Bhāskara. Salīm, p. 340, and Salīmullah (translated by Francis Gladwin under the title *A Narrative of the Transactions in Bengal During the Soobahdaries* [Calcutta: Stuart and Cooper, 1788], p. 107) agree that 'Alivardi was first surrounded outside the city but fought his way into the city and was besieged there. There is rough agreement with Gaṅgārām as to the siege itself. See Appendix II, p. 71.
48. Again Yusuf 'Ali's account varies (in *Bengal Nawābs*, p. 97):
"After some days had passed in this way, although the Nabāb wished to engage in an open field battle, yet as the Maratha war-tactics are flight and attack only when the enemy is off his guard, it could not come to pass. So he planned to leave his many things like wagons and carts in his camp and attack the Marathas with a select (light) force. . . ."
49. This is unusual; the term "*sahi*," used here, usually refers to servants of troopers—"syce," in charge of the horses. Perhaps here the term itself means troopers.

. . . pāe jāre //
baragira tarāse kehu bāhira nā hae /
catudige baragira ḍare rasada nā milae // 1
cāula kālāi maṭara muṣarī / 2
tela ghi āṭā cini labana eka sera kari //
ṭākā sera haila ānāja kintu nāi pāe /
khudra kāṅgāla jata mairā$_2$ jāe //
gājā bhāga tāmāka nā pāe kinite / 3
ānāja nāhi pāo(w)ā jāe lāgila bhābite //
kalāra āiṭhā jata yānila tuliyā /
tāhā āni saba loke khāe sijāiyā //
choṭa baṛa laskare jata loka chila /
kalāra āiṭhā sirddha saba loke khāila // 4
bisama bipatya baṛa biparita haila /
anya pare kā kathā nabāba sāheba khāila //
ei mate laskara āchila cauda roja /
tabe nabāba kuca kailā laiyā saba phauja //
ghoḍāra upare kata nisāna calila /
tabe ḍaṅkā nāgārā kata bājite lāgila //
jhākuḍa$_2$ kata sādiānā bājāe / 5
sāhisarā taba nabābera āge jāe //
cāirdige laskara cale nāi lekhājokhā /
hena kāle (catudige baragī dila dekhā) //

1. There is a scribal error; the MS reads /ḍare/; it should be read /tare/.
2. Mustaphi has /kalāi/.
3. Mustaphi has /bhāṅg/, the standard form of the word.
4. The MS is unclear; the proper reading may be /siddha/.
5. Mustaphi has /sādiyānā/.

appeared on all sides, with naked swords in their hands, and struck terror into the hearts of the Nabāb's men, who milled about in panic; and the baggage-carriers began to scream. Thousands upon thousands of Bargi horsemen drove down upon them with great speed [50] but were kept at a distance. Mustaphā Khān, with four companies of horse, rode firing volleys to drive off the Bargis.[51] The Bargis fled before him, but others encircled and attacked the Nabāb's rear. Mir Habib [52] was at that time in the rear guard; he was caught at a disadvantage by the Bargis and disappeared. [He joined forces with them.] The Bargis looted and plundered in the Nabāb's rear, laying waste the camp and all the tents and gear. They also captured many carts of treasure.[53] The Bargis came from all directions, and captured many horses and elephants and men. And many high-ranking soldiers quickly fled.

The Nabāb's men fled helter-skelter to Nikunsarā [Nigun Sarai],[54] and there Mosāheb Khān [55] was surrounded with all his horses and elephants.[56] When Mosāheb Khān was killed,

50. The term "*hānā hānā*" indicates the quickness of their movement. Apparently they were prevented from coming nearer by the Nawāb's artillery.

51. The text is not very clear at this point. The term "*dehaḍ maria*" probably means firing volleys. There is a portion of narrative here which seems to be absent from Gaṅgārām's version, though it is vital to the others. See *History of Bengal,* Vol. I, edited by Jadunath Sarkar (University of Dacca, 1948), p. 455. See Appendix II, p. 71.

52. Mīr Ḥabīb was a Persian peddler from Shirāz, who had become the right-hand man of Rastam Jang, son-in-law of Shujā-ud-din, whose son, Sarfarāz, 'Alivardi had killed in battle in 1740. This accounts for the enmity which he felt for 'Alivardi. For a longer account of Mīr Ḥabīb's antecedents, see Yusuf 'Ali's account in *Bengal Nawābs,* p. 99. See Appendix II, p. 72.

53. The text has "*khājānār gāṛi*" which may be translated as "carts carrying treasure chests." It was not unusual for the paymaster to move with the army, bringing the treasury with him.

54. About fourteen miles from Kāṭwā.

55. Yusuf 'Ali (*Bengal Nawābs,* p. 97) has: "That day there was severe fighting on both sides; in our army one chief, Musāhib Khān, the eldest son of 'Umar Khān, was slain." See Appendix II, p. 72.

56. There are two obscure lines here. The text uses the phrase "*ḍeṛa hātvir sāir.*" Kedarnāth Majumdār, who wrote more than fifty years ago, treated it as a specimen of East Bengal dialect used by the poet. He explained it as "row of many elephants." *Sāhitya pariṣad patrikā,* XV, p. 251.

. . . catudige baragī dila dekhā //
cāirdige baragī āila kata yāra /
tā sabhāra hāte dekhi lāhāṅgā tala(w)āra //
takhana nabābera laskare paila haṛabaṛa /
hena belā terahaināte dharilā ḍehaḍa // 1
hājāre$_2$ ghoṛā uṭhāe ekibāre /
hānā$_2$ kairā yāise kāchāite nāre // 2
tabe mustaphā khā̃ cāira hāra ghoḍā laiyā /
baragi khedāiyā jāe ḍehaṛa māriyā //
tabe sāmane haite baragī palāila /
āra kata baragi yāisā pichāṛi gherila // 3
mira habiba tabe pichāṛite chila /
bekābute paiṛā seha misāila //
pichāṛi luṭila baragi āsi yāra kata /
poḍāila ḍerāḍāṇḍā tāmbu jata //
khājānāra gāḍi jata sāte chila /
cāirdige baragi yāisā luṭite lāgila //
hāti ghoḍā kata luiṭā laiyā jāe /
baṛa baṛa sipāi jata umani palāe //
dauṛadauṛi āilā tabe nikunsarāe /
mosāheba khā̃ tabe paṛila gherāe //
deṛa hātvira māira haila tāra sāā / 4
pacisa gheḍā surddā kheta āila tāthe // 5
mosāheba khā̃ jadi paila nikunete /

1. The third word in the line could also read /tera haināte/ or /tera hailāte/.
2. Mustaphi reads /hārā hārā/, which is perhaps correct; see the note on the translation.
3. Mustaphi has /āila/ for /āisa/, but the MS is clear.
4. The line is difficult to read in MS; the translation is likewise unsatisfactory; Mustaphi reads /sāira/ for /māira/.
5. Scribal error for /ghoṛā/ is clear.

the Nabāb quickly made his way to Kāṭañā [Kāṭwā].[57] Hāji Sāheb[58] had sent supplies there by boat, and the men of the Nabāb ate, and were saved.[59]

When Bhāskara heard that the Nabāb had broken the siege and had reached Kāṭañā, he began to brood in this way: —Ah! They have escaped! All these days that I have surrounded them have been in vain.

Then the Bargis began to plunder the villages, and all the people fled in terror. Brahman *paṇḍits* fled, taking with them loads of manuscripts; goldsmiths fled with their scales and weights;[60] and petty traders fled with their wares, and coppersmiths with their coppers and brasses, and blacksmiths and potters, taking with them their wheels and equipment;[61] and fishermen of all kinds with their nets and lines, and conch-merchants with their tools—all fled. The people fled in all directions; who could count their numbers? Kāestas, Baidyas[62] —all who lived in villages fled, when they heard the name of the Bargis. Ladies of good family, who had never before set foot on road fled from the Bargis with baskets on their heads. And land-owning Rājputs, who had gained their wealth by

57. About 30 miles northwest of Burdwan, at the junction of the Bhāgirathī and Ajay rivers. J. C. K. Peterson (*Bengal District Gazetteer—Burdwan*, Calcutta, 1910) calls it "the key to Murshidabad."

58. I. e., Hāji Āhmad, the brother of the Nawāb, who was at that time encamped in Murshidabad. The Hāji had been one of the favorites of Shujā Khān, and one of that ruler's principal advisors (see *History of Bengal*, II, p. 437); he was instrumental in the instigation and in the success of 'Alivardi's victory over Sarfarāz and usurpation of the province. See Salīm, pp. 308-321; Yusuf 'Ali, *Bengal Nawābs*, pp. 84-90.

59. The account of Yusuf 'Ali differs somewhat in detail from this story of the Nawāb's dash to Kaṭwā. See Appendix II, p. 72.

60. The term used is "*haṛapi*," which is obscure.

61. The term "*naṛi*" is obscure.

62. I. e., Kāyasthas; a Hindu caste cluster. Baidya also indicates a cluster of castes, most of which practiced medicine.

jaldi nabāba sāheba yāilā kāṭa(w)āte [*sic*] //
ethāte hāji sāheba rasada laiñā /
pāṭhāiñā dila kata naikāe kariñā //
tabe rasada āsiyā kāṭañāte pahacila /
nabāba sāhebera loka khāiyā bācila //
gherāo haite nabāba āilā kaṭañāte [*sic*] /
śuniñā bhāskara tabe lāgilā bhābite //
chi chi chi hāe hāe gela palāiyā /
eta dina brathā āsiyā chilāũ gheriyā // 1
tabe saba baragi grāma luṭite lāgila /
jata grāmera loka saba palāila //
brāḥmana paṇḍita palāe pūthira bhāra laiyā /
sonāra bāinā palāe kata nikti haṛapi laiyā // 2
gandha banika palāe dokāna laiyā jata /
tāmā pitala laiyā kāsāri palāe kata //
kāmāra kumāra palāe laiyā cāka naṛi /
jāulā māuchā palāe laiyā jāla daṛi //
saṅka banika palāe karabha laiyā jata / 3
catudige loka palāe ki baliba kata //
kāesta baidya jata grāme chila /
baragira nāma suinā saba palāila //
bhāla mānusera śtriloka jata hāṭe nāi pathe /
baragīra palāne peṭāri lailā māthe //
kṣetri rājputa jata (tala(w)ārera dhani) /

1. Mustahpi reads /chilām/, but the MS is clear; the /-ũ/ suffix is an older form of the first person past.
2. The second word in the line is not clear.
3. Mustaphi reads /karā/ for /karabha/. End of the folio.

the sword, threw down their swords and fled.[63] And Gosañis[64] and Mohantas[65] fled, riding on litters, their bearers carrying bag and baggage on their shoulders; and many farmers and Kaibartas[66] fled, their seed for next year's crops on the backs of the bullocks, and plows on their shoulders. And all the Sekhs and Saiyads and Mogals and Pāṭhāns[67] who were in the villages fled when they heard the name of the Bargis. And pregnant women, all but unable to walk, began their labor on the road and were delivered there. And all the *sikdārs*[68] and village officials fled for their lives when they heard the name "Bargi."

There were some people who stood in the road and asked of all who passed where the Bargis were. Everyone replied:
—I have not seen them with my own eyes. But seeing everyone flee, I flee also.

So the poor and wretched people fled, their bundles of coarse and ragged clothing on their heads. There were old people with staffs in their hands, and Cāñis and Dhānuks[69] leading their

63. The text is obscure. The term "*dhani*" is the difficult one; alternative meanings might be "sound" (*dhvani*)—"the [empty] sounds of swords," or "decoration"—"whose swords were [mere] decoration." The phrase "*talayārera dhani*" might also mean something like "skilled with the sword."

64. I.e., *gosvāmi*. The term is usually used to designate a leader of the *Vaiṣṇava* sect or a highly respected person of Vaiṣṇava persuasion.

65. I.e., *mahānta*, the head of a *maṭh* or monastery, also usually Vaiṣṇava.

66. The name of a caste, at the present time a caste of fishermen.

67. These names indicate the ancestry of groups of Muslims in Bengal. Each of these groups has to some extent its own tradition and unity within the greater Muslim community.

68. Government official with police duties.

69. Names of tribal peoples.

. . . tala(w)ārera dhani /
tala(w)ār phelāiñā tārā palāna yamani //
gosañi mohanta jata caupālāra caṛiyā /
bocakā bucaki laya jata bāhuke kariyā //
cāsā kaibartta jata jāe palāiñā /
bichana bandera piṭhe ghāḍe lāṅgala laiyā // 1
seka saiyada mogala pāṭhāna jata grāme chila /
baragira nāma suinā saba palāila //
garbhabati nāri jata nā pāre calite /
dārūna bedanā pāiyā prasabiche pathe // 2
sikadāra pāṭāri jata grāme chila /
baragīra nāma suinā saba palāila //
dasa bisa loka yāisā pathe ḍāḍāilā /
tā sabhāre sodhāe baragi kothāe dekhenā //
tārā saba bole mora cakṣe dekhi nāi /
lokera palāla deikhā āmorā palāi //
kāṅgāla gariba jata jāe palāiñā /
kethā dhokaḍi kata māthāe kariñā //
buḍaburi jāe jata hāte laiyā naḍi /
cāñi dhānuka palāe kata chāgalera (galāe daṛi) //

1. /ghaḍe/ is omitted in Mustaphi's text.
2. Mustaphi reads /peye/ for /pāiyā/.

goats with ropes around their necks. From every village, big, or small, people fled in fear of the Bargis. People fled in four directions to various places. People of all thirty-six *varṇas* fled, and there was no end to their numbers.

But then suddenly the Bargis swept down with a great shout and surrounded the people in the fields. They stole all their gold and silver, leaving all other things aside. They cut off the hands of some, and the noses and ears of others. Some they cut down with a single blow. They seized and dragged off the most beautiful of the women, who tried to flee, and tied ropes around their fingers and necks. When one had finished with a woman, another took her, while the raped women screamed for help. The Bargis did many foul and bestial things to the women, and then let them go.[70] Then, when they had plundered all they could in the fields, they entered the villages and set fire to large houses. *Bāṅgāla*,[71] *Chāuāri*,[72] *Viṣṇu maṇḍapas*[73] —they burned them all, large and small. They destroyed whole

70. Unchastity, even when forced, could mean for a woman a life of misery.

71. Bungalows.

72. Thatch-roofed houses.

73. Pavilions for worship or celebration.

. . . galāe daṛi //
choṭa baṛa grāme jata loka chila /
baragira bhae saba palāila //
cāirdige loka palāe ṭhāñiṭhāñi /
charttisa barñe loka palāe tāra anta nāñi // 1
ei mate saba loka palāiyā jāite /
ācambite baragi gherila āisā tāthe //
māṭhe gheriyā baragi deya tabe sāḍā /
sonārūpā luṭe āra nee saba chāḍā //
kārū hāta kāṭe karū nāka kāna /
eki coṭe kāru badhae paṛāna // 2
bhāla$_2$ śtrīloka jata dhairā laiyā jāe /
āṅgusṭhe daḍi bādhi dee tāra galāe //
eka janā chāḍe tāre āra janā dhare /
ramanera bhare trāhi sabda kare //
ei mate baragi saba kata pāpa karmma kairā / 3
sei saba śtriloke jata dee saba chāiṛā //
tabe māṭhe luṭīyā baragi grāme sādhāe /
baṛa$_2$ ghare āisā āguni lāgāe //
bāṅgālā cauāri jata bisṇū moṇḍaba /
choṭa baḍa ghara ādi poḍāilā saba //
ei mate jata saba grāma poḍāiyā /

1. Second word in the line unclear in MS.
2. Mustaphi reads /parāna/.
3. Fourth word in the line unclear; possibly the scribe intended to cross it out.

villages and swept, looting, into all the four directions. They bound some people, their hands behind their backs, others they threw to the ground and while they were on their backs on the ground, kicked them with shoes.[74] They shouted over and over again, " Give us money! ", and when they got no money they filled peoples' nostrils with water, and some they seized and drowned in tanks, and many died of suffocation. In this way they did all manner of foul and evil deeds. When they demanded money and it was not given to them, they would put the man to death. Those who had money gave it. Those who had none were killed.

In the Tretā Age[75] there lived a king named Bhagiratha. By the power of his austerities he brought the Ganges to earth; because of this the Ganges is known as the Bhāgirathī.[76] It was on the other side[77] of this Bhāgirathī that the people found deliverance. Listen carefully now to the names of the villages which the Bargis razed:

Candrakonā, Medinipur, Diganpur,[78] Khirapāi, they burnt, and Bardhamān city; Nimagāchi, Seṛagā, Simailā, Caṇḍipur, Śyāmpur, and Anailā-grām. In this way they razed [the dis-

74. One of the greatest indignities which can be visited upon a person in India.

75. The second Age of the world, in the traditional chronology.

76. Bhāgirathī is another name for the Ganges. Here the river Hughli, a branch of the Ganges, is meant. From the point at which the Hughli branches off from the main stream the latter loses its sanctity, and the Hughli is considered as " the real and much-venerated Ganges."

77. I. e., on the eastern side of the river. Salīm (pp. 343-344) has:

" The wealthy nobility and gentry, to save their family honor, quitted their homes and migrated across the Ganges. The whole tract from Akbarnagar (Rajmahal) to Mednipur and Jalisar (Jalasore) came into the possession of the Mahrattas. Those murderous freebooters drowned in the rivers a large number of the people, after cutting off their ears, noses, and hands. Tying sacks of dirt to the mouths of others, they mangled and burnt them with indescribable tortures. Thus they desolated and dishonored the family and children of a whole world."

78. Dīganagar?

caturdige baragi beḍāe luṭīyā //
kāhuke bādhe baragi diyā piṭhamoḍā /
cita kairā māre lāthi pāe jutā caṛā //
rupi diha$_2$ bole bārebāre /
rūpi nā pāiyā tabe nāke jala bhare //
kāhuke dhariyā baragī pakhaire ḍūbāe /
phāphara haiñā tabe kārū prāna jāe //
ei mate baragi kata biparita kare /
ṭākā kaṛi nā pāile tabe prāne mare //
jāra ṭākā kaṛi āche se dee baragire /
jāra ṭākā kaṛi nāi sei prāne mare //
tretā juge rājā bhagiratha chilā /
aneka tapasyā kari gaṅgā yānilā // 1
pṛthibite nāma tāra haila bhāgirathi /
tāra pāra haiyā loke pāila abyāhati //
tabe kona kona grāma baragi dila poṛāiñā /
se saba grāmera nāme suna mona diyā //
candrakonā medanipura āra diganagara /
khirapāi poḍāe āra barddhamāna sahara //
nimagāchi seṛagā āra simailā /
caṇḍipūra syāmapūra grāma ānailā //

1. The first word in the line is unclear.

trict of] Bardhamān in all four directions, and came to the port of Hugli. Pir Khān was then *phaujdār*[79] in Hugli, and because of him the Bargis could not plunder that city. They plundered Sātsaikā, Rājabāṭī, Cāndpur, Kāthārā-Sarāi, Ḍāmadvāi, Jadupur, Bhāṭachālā, Merajāpur, Cāndaṛā, Kuṛaban, Pālāsi [Plassey], Bauci, Beṛaṛā, Samurddhagaṛa, Jānnagar, Nadiyā, Māhātāpur, Sūnanṭapur Thail—all these were burned. Parāṇapur, Bhāṭarā, Māndaṛā, Saradāṅgā, Dhitapur, Cāndaṛagrām, Sātsaikā, Jāgirābād, Kumirā, Baultali, and Nimadā were burned, as were Kaṛai, Baithan, Cāṛaila, Siṅgi, Bāskā, Ghiṛānā, Mastaila, Goṭapāṛā,[80] Cāndapāṛā, and Jāgadiyā. During the night they set fire to Patli. And they destroyed Ātāihāṭ, Pātāihāṭ, Ḍāñihāṭ,[81] Beṛā-bhāosiṃha, Bikihāṭ, and looted the Indrāilparganā, Kāgā, Mogā, and the factories of the Dutch people.[82] After burning Kāgā and Mogā, they swept on by night to Jāumākāndi,[83] and began to plunder the Birbuiparganā.[84] They set up outposts at Amaḍharā and Maheserpur, and Gowālābhūñi and Senabhūñi—all were destroyed. They razed everything in their path until they came to Biṣṇupur. But Gopāl defended Bonabiṣṇupur and against him the Bargis

79. *Phaujdār.* Wilson, *Glossary*: "An officer of the Mogul government, who was invested with the charge of the police and jurisdiction in all criminal matters. A criminal judge, a magistrate. The chief of a body of troops."

Jadunath Sarkar says, "*Mahārāshtra Purāṇ* wrongly speaks of Sher Khān as *faujdar* of Hughli." In the *Sāhitya pariṣad patrikā* printed version of the text (p. 224), the name of the *faujdar* was "Sher Khān," while "Pir Khān" occurs in the manuscript. Sarkar also points out that in the *Siyār-ul-Mutākẖerīn* the name given is "Md. Yar Khan, reputed brother of Alivardi, popularly called Mirza Piare." (Sarkar, *Fall of the Mughal Empire,* Vol. I, p. 84 fn.) Gaṅgārām was apparently referring to him. For Yusuf 'Ali's and Salīm's accounts see p. 73.

80. About 25 miles west of Plassey.
81. A town of the Kāṭwā subdivision on the right bank of the Bhāgirathī.
82. The major Dutch settlements at this period were at Cinsura.
83. I. e., Jemuyā Kāndī.
84. I. e., Birbhum.

ei mate barddhamāna poṛāe cāira bhite /
punarapi āilā baragi bandhara hugalite //
pira khā̃ pha̐ujadāra tabe hugalite chila / 1
tāhāra kārane baragī luṭīte nārila //
sāta saikā rājabāṭī āra cāndrapūra /
kāhārā sabāi ḍāmadvai jadupura // 2
bhāṭachālā poṛāe āra merajāpūra cāndaṛā /
kuṛabana palāsi yāra bouci beḍaṛā //
samurddharagaṛa jārnnagara āra nadiyā /
māhātāpura sūnanṭapura thaila poḍāe giyā //
parānapura bhāṭarā poṛāe āra mādaṛā /
saraḍāṅgā dhitapura āra grāma cāndaḍā // 3
sāta saikā jāgirābāda sakala poḍāiñā /
kumirā baulatali nimadā poḍāe giñā //
kaḍai kaithala poṛāe āra cāṛaila /
siṅgi bāskā ghoṛānāsa mastaila //
goṭapāṛā cādapāṛā āra yāgadiyā /
rātārāti pāṭali dila poṛāiyā //
ātāihāṭa pātāihāṭa yāra ḍāñihāṭa /
beṛābhāo siṃha poṛāe āra bikīhāṭa //
ei rūpe indrāila paraganā baragi luṭi /
kāgāe mogāe luṭe olendejera kuṭi //
ei rūpe kāgā̃ mogā̃ poḍāiñā /
rātarāti pahacilā jāumākāndi giñā //
tabe birabhui paraganā baragi dila poḍāiñā /
āmaḍaharā mahaserapura thānā kaila giñā //
go(w)ālābhuiñi senabhuñi saba poḍāila /
catudiga poṛāiyā biṣṇupūra āila //
tabe bonabiṣṇupura gopāla rakṣā kare /

1. End of folio.
2. Mustaphi reads /katthārā sarāi/, and the scribe's hand is such that either reading is possible.
3. Mustaphi reads /sarabhāṅgā/; the scribe's hand is not clear.

could do nothing; it was beyond their power.[85] The Bargis then rushed to loot the cities of Naihāṭi and Urddhānpur, keeping Kātañā to the right.[86] They crossed the Bāblā river[87] and came to Māṅganapāṛa, Sāṭai,[88] and Kāmanagar; they passed through Mahulā, Caurigāchā, and Kāthāliyā, and came to Ādhāramānika by way of Rāṅgamāiṭā.[89] They burst upon Go(w)ālajān, Badhuipāṛā, Neyālisapāṛā, and swiftly reached Dāhāpāṛā. The Choṭa Nabāb Hāji Sahib was on the other bank of the river, but when he heard the name of the Bargis he retreated quickly into his fort.[90] Then the Bargis crossed over at Hājigañj-ghāṭ, and swiftly moved and plundered the house of Jagat Seṭ;[91] they took all the Arcot rupees[92] that were in the house, and filled their horsefodder containers with money and carried it off, scattering two or three hundred rupees behind them. Quickly they crossed again to the other bank of the Ganges. The householders and the fakirs scrambled for the money they had left.[93]

The Nabāb Sāheb, who was then at Kāṭañā, heard of these things, and that the Bargis had looted the house of Jagat Seṭ.

85. For a curious account of this episode, see *Appendix* I.

86. Urddhānpur is about five miles above Kāṭwā. Naihāṭi is about 25 miles from Calcutta.

87. The Bāblā River flows northward through *thānas* Mayreswar and Ranpurhat and then turns east into Murshidabad district; also known as Dwarka. (*Birbhum District Gazetteer.*)

88. In central Birbhum district, on the Mor River.

89. I. e., Rāṅgāmāṭī.

90. This seems to be the foray of Mīr Ḥabīb into Murshidabad which is also mentioned later on. For Salīm's account, see p. 73.

91. The Seṭs (Seths) are one of the most interesting families in all Bengal, and some space might be taken here to treat their history in some detail. See p. 73.

92. N. K. Sinha in his *Economic History of Bengal* (Vol. I, p. 119) refers to this. See p. 75.

93. "*Phakir-phakīrā*" would mean faqirs and other such people. "Faqir" is a Muslim mendicant.

Scattering of money to create confusion or prevent pursuit was a well-known ruse. For more on this, see p. 75.

yasādya baragira tabe kī karite pāre //
sahara luṭīte baragī tabe āila dhāiyā /
naihāṭi urddhānapura kāṭañā ḍāhine thuiyā //
bābalā nadi baragi tabe pāra haila /
māṅgalapāḍā sāṭai kāmanagara āila //
mahulā caurigāchā āra kāṭhaliyā /
ādhāramānika āilā baragi rāṅgāmāiṭā diyā //
go(w)ālajāna budhaipāḍā āra ne(w)ālisapāḍā /
sigragati yāsiyā pahacilā dāhāpāṛā //
hāji choṭa nabāba upāre chila /
baragira nāma suinā kīllāe sādhāila //
tabe baragi pāra hailā hājigañjera ghāṭe / 1
sigragati āisā jagata seṭera bāṛi luṭe //
āḍakāṭa ṭākā jata ghare chila /
ghoḍāṛa khuraci bhairā saba ṭākā nila // 2
tabe sao dui tina ṭākā chiṭāiñā / 3
sigragati gelā baragī gaṅgā pāra haiyā // 4
tabe phakiraphakīrā girasta jata chila /
sei saba ṭākā tārā luṭite lāgila //
tabe kāṭañāte nabāba sāheba sunila /
jagata seṭera bāḍi baragi luiṭā gela //

1. The MS is badly creased at this point, and the second and third words in the line could not be deciphered in the photostatic copy from which we were working. We have therefore followed Mustaphi's readings here and below.
2. The first word in the line must be a scribal error for /ghoṛāra/.
3. Mustaphi reads /chaṛāiyā/, but the MS is clear.
4. The MS is creased; therefore the third and fourth words are unclear.

As soon as the messenger had given him the news, the Nabāb moved quickly out from Kāṭañā. He marched silently, by night, and by dawn had reached Monakarā. There he berated the Hāji severely, that though the Hāji had had a strong army there he had still allowed the city to be looted.

When the Nabāb Sāheb had come to his fort, the Bargis had assembled in strength at Kāṭañā. It was then the month of Āṣāṛh,[94] and the clouds were rumbling ceaselessly. The rains were heavy. The flooding Ajay had filled the Ganges to overflowing, and the Bargis were able to loot no longer. So, surrounding Kāṭañā, Bhāosiṃha-berā, and Ḍāihāṭ,[95] they had pitched their camps on all sides. The *jamidārs* [*zamindārs*] of all the villages around had come to Bhāskara, and *tāgidārs*[96] were sent to villages to press for rent.

Hear now of the doings of Mir Habib:

Mir Habib built a bridge of boats, and had ordered that all the large boats which could be pressed into service be brought, had had them lashed together side by side and had run a pole from one bank of the river to the other. Then he

94. June-July, the third month of the calendar. It is the time when the first monsoon comes to Bengal.

95. I. e., Ḍāñihāṭ—see note 81 above.

96. Petty revenue officers.

eteka kathā jadi harakārā kahila /
kāṭañā haite nabāba śighra calila // 1
rātārātī tabe nabāba āilā monakarā /
bhora haite haite tabe pahacilā ḍerā //
tabe hāji sāhebake nabāba yaneka bulila /
eteka laskara raite bāḍi luiṭā gela //
nabāba sāheba jadi āilā kīllāte /
tabe saba baragi jaḍa haila kāṭañāte //
āsāṛa māsera deo(w)ā ghana barisana / 2
ajae bhāsiyā gaṅgā bharila takhana //
gaṅgā bharila jadi ipāra upāra /
tabe baragi luṭībāre nāhi pāe āra //
kāṭañā bhāosiṃha beḍā ḍāihāṭa niyā /
cāidige baragi chāyani kaila giyā //
grāme$_2$ jata jamidāra chila /
tāra sabe āsi bhāskake mililā //
grāme$_2$ jata tāgidāra gela /
tārā saba jāiyā khājānā sādite lāgila //
ethā mira habiba laiyā kīchu suna bibaraṇa /
pharāsabandira parttana karilā takhana //
baṛa$_2$ naukā jekhane jata chila /
begāra dhariyā saba naukā ānila //
ipāre upāre lāhāsa dila tānāiyā /
naukā saba tāra madhye rākhi bāndhiyā // 3

1. Last two words indecipherable: the MS is creased. We have followed Mustaphi, though the form /śighra/ is unlikely.
2. Mustaphi reads /bariṣaṇa/.
3. The folio ends with this line.

had had bamboo brought from all the surrounding villages and, having lashed it all together, had made of it a deck on top of the boats; and over it all he had had grass mats spread, and scattered baskets of earth, and then had had it all levelled off. Then the horsemen rode across it by the thousands. When this bridge was completed at the Ḍāihāṭ-ghāṭ, the Bargi cavalry rode across it, bent on plunder.

But hear also of the doings of Bhāskara, as he began *pūjā*[97] at Ḍāihāṭ. As many *zamindārs* as there were in the surrounding villages he summoned to his camp, and said to them:

—I want now to perform *pūjā* to the Mother of the World.[98]

This Bhāskara told them and in devotion the *zamindārs* began to make preparations. They ordered image-makers to prepare the image,[99] and the image-makers duly made the image and left the place. They brought hundreds of loads of all kinds of sweets and delicacies. Bhāskara will perform *pūjā*; therefore goats and buffaloes by the thousands were brought for the sacrifice. Thus did Bhāskara prepare for his *pūjā*.

97. Refers to *Durgāpūjā*, the worship of goddess Dūrgā, the most popular festival in Bengal. It takes place in autumn and lasts for three days.

98. I. e., Durgā.

99. For the worship of Durgā an image of straw and earth is made. It depicts the goddess carrying weapons in her ten hands and slaying a demon, which is the spirit of evil. On the fourth day the image is taken to a river or tank for immersion.

grāme$_2$ haite āne jata bāsa /
naukāra upara bichāiya bāddhena pharāsa //
ghāsa cāṭāi tāra upare ta dila /
pāichāe$_2$ māṭī phelite lāgila //
māṭī pheliyā tabe kare barābara /
hājāre$_2$ ghoḍā jāe tāra upara //
ḍāñihāṭera ghāṭe jadi pūla bādhā gela /
kata sata baragi tārā luṭite calila //
ethā bhāskara laiyā kichu suna bibarana /
jerupe ḍāñihāṭe kaila pūjā ārambhana //
tabe grāme$_2$ jata jamidāra chila /
tā sabhāre ḍāka diyā nikaṭe ānila //
kahite lāgila tabe tā sabhāra ṭhāñi /
jagatajanani māera pūjā karite cāi //
ei kathā bhāskara kahila tā sabhāre /
śraddhā pāiyā tārā saba urjoga kare // 1
ghaṭakarpura āne kehu kariyā sanmāna //
āsiñā pratimā tārā karena nirmmāna //
ei rūpe kumāra pratimā bānāiyā /
bhāskarera ṭhāi tārā gela bidāe haiyā //
tāra pare upādae sāmagri āila jata /
bhāra bāhāndhite bojhāe kata sata //
bhāskara karibe pujā bali dibāra tare /
chāga mahisa āise kata hājāre$_2$ //
ei mate kare bhāskara pujā yārambhana /

1. Next to last word not clear in MS.

Meanwhile, Mir Habib, with many Bargis, had set out over the bridge which they had built. Riding by night, they reached Phuṭisāko.[100] In the second watch of the night a great outcry arose, and from it the Nabāb learned that the Bargis were at Phuṭisāko. The Nabāb sent a messenger. The messenger ran quickly in the second watch of the night and, reaching the troops, said to them repeatedly:

—Make ready to ride, by command of the Nabāb!

When the messenger said this, all saddled their horses, and the *jamādārs* began to prepare [for battle]. The drums began to beat, and Mustaphā Khān and Samsera Khān, these two *jamādārs*, rode forth with twenty thousand horse. Raham Khān and Karam Khān also rode out, and ten thousand horse rode swiftly with them. Ātāullā and Mir Jāfar readied themselves for battle and rode at the head of fifteen thousand horse. Umar Khān and Āsālat went forth with five thousand horse. Ṭhākursiṃha and the *baksi bahaniyā*[101] went, taking with them forty thousand equipment bearers. Phate Hāji and Chedan Hāji went with thirty-five thousand. There were, then, sixty

100. It seems possible that this is the same raid by Mīr Ḥabīb on Murshidabad mentioned earlier in the text. Salīm (p. 341) mentions as the reason for Mīr Ḥabīb's raid that Mīr S̲harif, his brother, and his family, and the family treasure, were there. Salīm also says that there were seven hundred cavalry with him on the expedition.

101. *Baksi* is a deviant form of the word usually spelled bakshi. Wilson's *Glossary* has: "A paymaster, an officer whose special duty it was also to keep an account of all disbursements connected with military tenures, as those of *Mansubdars* and *Jagirdars*. Paymaster of the forces, under the Mughal system, frequently one with the Commander-in-Chief."
"*Bahaniyā*" means a carrier. Perhaps here "*baksi bahaniyā*" means an officer in charge of the baggage carriers.

ethā mira habiba baragī laiyā karila gamana //
tabe baragi pharāsabandite pāra haiyā /
rātārāti phuṭisāko uṭhilena giyā //
dutiya prahara rāite haḍabaḍi haila / 1
phuṭisāka baragi āila nabāba sunila //
tabe nabāba sāheba nakība pāṭhāe /
dutiya prahara rāite nakība sigra dhāe //
nakība āsiñā tabe bole bāra$_2$ /
hukuma nabābera sayāri karaha taiyāra //
eteka kahila jadi nakība āsiñā /
tabe saba ghoṛāe jina dila caḍāiñā //
eke$_2$ jamādāra lāgila sājite /
ḍaṅkā nāgārā kata lāgila bājite // 2
mustaphā khā̃ samasera khā dui jamādāra /
jāra saṅge jāe ghoḍā bisa hājāra // 3
rahama khā̃ karama khā̃ dui janāte jāe /
dasa hājāra ghoḍā jāra saṅge dhāe //
ātāullā mira jāphara duijanā sājila /
ponera hājāra ghoḍā saṅge calila //
umara khā̃ āsālata duijanāte gela /
pāca hājāra ghoḍā saṅge kairā nila //
ṭhākur siṅha jāe āra baksi bahaniyā / 4
callisa hājāra bahaniyā saṅgeta kariyā //
phate hāji chedana hāji dui janāte gela /
peetisa hājāra bahaniyā saṅge calila //
sāiṭa hājāra ghoḍā (ḍeḍalāka bahaniyā) /

1. Mustaphi reads /duitya/.
2. The second word in the line is unclear.
3. Mustaphi has both /jāe/ and /yāe/; the MS has both, but /yāe/ is crossed out.
4. The first word in the line is unclear.

thousand horse and one hundred and fifty thousand carriers.[102] The Nabāb advanced to Tārakpur with this great army.

As soon as the Nabāb came to Tārakpur the Bargis saw the strength[103] of his force and retreated. They turned their backs and ran, with the army of the Nabāb at their heels. There were many Bargi camps at Palāsi [Plassey], and they left these camps and fled, when they heard the name of the Nabāb. They fled swiftly across their bridge, and reached Kāṭañā. The Nabāb, marching by night, came to Rahanpur, saw that the Bargis were encamped at Kāṭañā. The Nabāb gave orders for batteries to be set up at Rahanpur and he placed his artillery to cover all the four directions. Then he wrote letters to Pūraniyā and Pāṭanā,[104] and two men came, when they heard the account.

Jayandi Āhmad Khān[105] came from Pāṭanā with twelve thousand horse, and the Nabāb Bāhādur[106] came from Pūraniyā, bringing five thousand troops with him. Then Jayandi Āhmad said to the Nabāb:

—Strike Bhāskara before the *pūjā* is finished.

But the Nabāb said:

—Let the Dasarā pass first.[107] Let us wait until all the mud and water are dried up. That will be better.

102. The figures given in the text add up to fifty thousand horse and seventy-five thousand "carriers." The total in the text is sixty thousand horse and one hundred and fifty thousand "carriers." The poet apparently does not mention all the officers and their troops.

103. "*dhamak*" literally means threat.

104. The Nawāb's nephews, who were also his sons-in-law, were his deputies in Purnea and Patna. They now came to his aid.

105. I.e., Zainuddin, the son of Hājī Āhmad, thus the nephew of the Nawāb. He was the father of Sirāj-ud-daulah, whom the English defeated at Plassey in 1757. Yusuf 'Ali refers to this. See p. 75.

106. Nawāb Bāhādur refers to Saif Khān of Purnea, a nephew and son-in-law of 'Alivardi.

107. I.e., Dussera, the fourth or last day of the *pūjā*, when the image is taken in procession and immersed. The period after Dussera was considered suitable for military campaign. The Marathas usually began their campaigns on the Dussera day or soon after.

. . . ḍeḍalāka bahaniyā /
tārakapūra āilā nabāba eta phauja laiyā //
jei mātra nabāba sāheba tārakapura āila /
phaũjera dhamaka deikhā baragi pichāila //
tabe baragi piṭha diyā sigra cailā jāe /
nabāba sāhebera phaũja piche$_2$ dhāe //
palāsite jata baragira thānā chila /
nabāba sāhebera nāma suinā umani palāila //
sigrati āsi baragi pule pāra haila /
pāra haiñā pūla tabe kāṭiñāta dila //
ethā nabāba rātārāti āilā rahapure /
dekhe baragira chāoni kāṭañāra upare //
rahanapure nabāb sāheba moracā dila /
catudige topakhā rūpiyā rākhila //
pūraniñā pāṭanāe lekhilena khata /
calilā duijanā śuinā hakikata //
ethā jayandi āhāmmada khā̃ āilā pāṭanā haite / 1
bāra hājāra ghoṛa phaũja laiyā sāthe //
nabāba bāhādura āilā pūraniñā haite /
pāca hājāra phaũja seha laiyā sāthe //
tabe jayandi āhammada bole nabābake /
pūjā nā haite āge māra bhāskarake //
nabāba bole yāge dasarā jāūka /
cāira dige jana kādā sakali śukāuka //

1. Folio ends with this line.

Jayandi Āhmad replied:

—When the mud and water are dried up, the Bargis will again be strong and will again begin to loot and plunder the country and burn everything. Let us ferry the troops by boats to the other side of the river; they can take the Bargis by night by surprise.

Thus did Jayandi Āhmad advise the Nabāb. But hear of Mir Habib's actions in the meantime:

Mir Habib had great cannon brought and arranged in rows in a boat which he had brought from Hugli. The gunners began their fire, and the shot tore the breastworks and fell upon the Nabāb's troops. As the balls fell on the army, the Nabāb's men retreated. But, while firing, a cannon burst and sank the boat, its bottom in splinters. Ten or twenty men were drowned, and others were killed by the bursting of the gun. And when he heard that he had lost both boat and cannon, Mir Habib began to think:

—There is no victory! I prepared so carefully and well, and still I have failed.

eta jadi nabāba bulilā tāra tare /
jayandi āhāmmada khā bole nabābere //
jana kādā sukhāile baragira habe bala /
catudige luṭibe poḍābe sakala //
phauja pāra kairā di naukāe kariyā /
rātārātī jena baragi māre giyā //
jayandi āhāmmada nabāba ei mansubā kare /
mira habiba laiñā kichu śuna tāra pare //
baḍa baḍa kāmāna āilā thuilā thare$_2$ / 1
hugali haite sulupha yāne tāra pare //
tabe golandāje golā sāgite lāgila /
moracā chediyā golā phāũje paṛila //
jei mātra golā āisā phāũje paila /
takhana nabāba sāhebera loka umani pichāila //
golā dāgite kāmāna gela phuiṭā /
sulupha ḍubila talā tāra phāiṭā //
dasa bisa loka tārā nikaṭe chila /
kāmāna phāṭīñā dui cāirajanā maila //
sulupha kāmāna jadi dui tabe gela /
suniñā mira habiba tabe bhābite lāgila //
phate nai$_2$ bole bāre$_2$ /
eteka urjaga karilāma nārilāu jinibāre // 2

1. Mustaphi reads /thare ghare/.
2. Mustaphi reads /nārilām/.

The sun was setting, then, and darkness descending. Hear now what the Nabāb did:

When the messengers came running to him with the news that the cannon had burst, the Nabāb gained heart, and ordered his army to advance. His troops, which were then in retreat, returned to their batteries. The battle torches were lit and thousands of musketeers flocked to the battery. Thousands of guns were fired in volleys, and the Bargis stood and gaped, on the other shore. They looked [back] upon the army of the Nabāb, drawn up in force.

Thus the troops of the Nabāb were stationed. Jayandi Āhmad Khān, meanwhile, had arrived at Uddharanpur with large boats.[108] These boats he began to lash together to construct a bridge. Over this bridge a great part of his force crossed at Uddharanpur. They advanced to the banks of the Ajay. Again they built a bridge, and ten thousand men marched across in silence; Ratan Hajari with two thousand two hundred troops were on the boats. But when they had reached the middle, [the bridge] burst asunder and many men were drowned.[109]

108. The phrase used is "*baṛa baṛa pāṭeli.*" "*Pāṭeli*" is a large river boat used for the transportation of cargo.

109. Salīm, as usual, has a somewhat variant description of the episode (p. 345): ". . . Mahābat Jang marched expeditiously with a large and efficient army, and by forced marches, at midnight reached a place just opposite to Katwāh. In the cover of the night's darkness, he instantly floated a bridge of boats that had been kept ready from before, and with a large army commenced crossing the river. Whilst he with the officers and some veteran soldiers had crossed the river, the bridge suddenly gave way under the weight of a large army. Some of the boats sank, whilst a large number of Afghāns and Bhalīahs were drowned in the river."

suryya astta gela sandhyā haila takhana /
ethā nabāba laiñā kichu śuna bibarana //
sambāda laiñā harakārā āila hāiṭā //
kahila nabābe kāmāna gela phāiṭā //
eteka suniñā nabābe haila bala /
hukuma karilā phā̃uje āṅgāuka sakala //
jata laskara tārā piche haiṭā chila /
āpana$_2$ moracāe sabhāi āila //
tabe bala māhātāba saba jāliyāta dila /
bara kandājera parā moracāe lāgila //
hājāre$_2$ āo(w)āja hae ekibāre /
ḍāṛāiñā baragi saba dekhe upāre //
ei mate nabābera phā̃uja āche barābare /
ethā jayandi āhāmma khā̃ āilā uddhāranapure // 1
baṛā$_2$ pāṭeli sāthe āilā chila /
juḍindā bādhiyā gudārā lāgāila //
urddhrānapūre jata phauja pāra kailā /
yajaera dhāre āisā saba ḍāḍāilā //
punarapi juḍindā yāilā lāgāila /
dasa hājāra phauja nisabde pāra haila //
bāisa sao loka surddhā ratana hājāri /
pāṭelira upare tārā sabhe caḍi //
jei mātra pāṭeli āila madhyakhāne /
talā phāṭīyā ḍubila sei sthāne //

1. Clearly a scribal error for /āhāmmad/.

When the boat sank, a great outcry arose among the troops. Hearing the outcry, the Bargis discovered the maneuver [which Jayandi Āhmad was attempting]. The cry went up in the Bargi camp that the Mogāls[110] were coming, and the Bargis threw themselves upon their horses and fled headlong. In the Bargi army there was great confusion, and the baggage carriers began to scream. Two Bargis were mounted upon each horse, as they fled. They abandoned their goods and supplies. And Bhāskara himself fled, though he had completed only the Saptami and Aṣṭami of the *pūjā*,[111] and he left the image behind him. The bearers then looted all the sweetmeats and other goods which were there, and took all the goats and fish and buffaloes. They took all the goods, while Bhāskara fled with his army. After Bhāskara had fled to a distance, Jayandi Āhmad Khān learned of his flight. Joyful music was played and alms were distributed to all the fakirs.[112]

It was in the month of Āśvin that Bhāskara fled. He returned again in Caitra, ready for battle.[113] The *sardār*[114] called all his men together and said to them:

110. The term "*mogāl*" is used generally in the sense of Muslims; the predominantly Hindu Marathas would not discriminate.

111. I.e., the first two days of the *pūjā* (seventh and eighth of the month; the third day is called "*navami*" (ninth); the fourth day is the "*dasami*" or "*dasera*" (tenth), when the image is immersed.

112. The line reads: "*phakira phukrāke*," fakirs and others.

113. Caitra is the month March-April, the last month of the calendar year. The affair was not as simple as Gaṅgārām would lead us to believe. Many strange events occurred between the time when Bhāskara was driven from Bengal and the time when he returned. For Yusuf 'Ali's account, see p. 75.

114. "*Sardār*," chief, refers to Bhāskara himself, as will be evident from the following lines.

pāṭeli ḍubila phaũje haila kalaraba /
upāre baragīra phaũje jānilā saba //
mogalā āila$_2$ paila haḍabaḍi /
takhana ghoṛāe caḍiyā baragi jāe dauṛādauṛi //
baragira laskare jadi paila haṛabaṛa /
hena kāle bahaināte dharilā ḍehaḍa //
eka eka ghoṛāe dui$_2$ baragi caṛiyā /
darya sāmagri kata jāe phelāiyā // 1
saptami aṣṭami dui pujā kari /
bhāskara palāiyā jāe pratimā chāḍi //
miṣṭānna sāmagri jata chila kāche /
bahaniyā luṭite lāgila tāra pāche //
chāga matsa maisa tāhā jata chila / 2
bahaniyā āsiyā saba luṭite lāgila //
ei mate sāmagri luṭe bahaniyā /
hotā phaũja laiyā bhāskara gela palāiyā //
bhāskara palāiyā jadi gela yaneka dure /
jayandi yāhāmmada khā sunila tāra pare //
sādiyānā nahabata kata bājhe thare$_2$ / 3
phakira phukarāke khaerāta kata kare //
āsvina māse bhāskara gela palāiyā /
caitra māse punarūpi āila sājiyā //
jei mātre punarapi bhāskara āila /
tabe saradāra sakalake ḍākīyā kahila //

1. Mustaphi reads /drabya/, which is preferable.
2. Second word in the line is unclear.
3. End of folio; next to last word in the line is unclear.

—Go, and cut down with your sword every man and woman whom you see.

As the *sardār* said this, his men went forth looting and killing in all directions, and shouting, "Kill!" Every Brahman or Vaiṣṇava or *sannyāsi* whom they saw they killed, and they slaughtered cows and women by the hundreds.[115] They did many evil things in this way.

When she saw the dire straits of the people, Pārvatī[116] was very angry. Paśupati [Siva] ordered that the sinners should be killed. The evil-minded ones had killed Brahmans and Vaiṣṇavas.

Saṅkarī[117] was also angry, and said:

—I cannot countenance such injury to Brahmans and Vaiṣṇavas.

There were around her many Bhairavīs,[118] and Yoginīs,[119] making gestures of obeisance with joined hands, standing in front of her. Saṅkarī spoke to them in this way:

—Hear, O Bhairavīs. Be hostile to Bhāskara; be gracious toward the Nabāb.

And when she had said this, Durgā went away. Hear now how Bhāskara was killed.

115. Salīm (p. 347) has: "Bhāskara Pandit, after his defeat, sent *bairagi* dacoits toward Akbarnagar (Rajmahal). . . ."

116. Pārvatī, another name for Durgā, so called because she was believed to be daughter of the Himalayas. *Parvata* in Sanskrit means "mountain."

117. I. e., "She who is beneficent," Pārvatī.

118. *Bhairavī*, generally a name of Durgā, one of her fourteen manifestations. In Bengali literature the term is often used in the sense of an attendant of Durgā, one having supernatural power, a female Tantric ascetic. The term is also used to refer to a female devotee of Bhairava (Śiva).

119. Yoginīs are also female Tantric ascetics. M. Monier-Williams, *Sanskrit-English Dictionary*, has: "A female demon or any being endowed with magical power . . . sorcerers (represented as eight in number and as created by Durgā and attendant on her or on Śiva; sometimes 60, 64 or 65 are enumerated)."

stri pūrūsa ādi kari jateka dekhibā / 1
tala(w)āra khuliyā saba tāhāre kāṭibā //
eteka bacana jadi balila saradāra /
catudige luṭe kāṭe bole māra māra //
brāḥmaṇa baiṣṇaba jata sanyāsi chila /
gohatyā strihatyā sata$_2$ kaila //
hājāre$_2$ pāpa kaila durammati /
lokera bipatya deikhā rūsilā pārbbati // 2
pāpiṣṭa mārite ādesilā pasupati /
braḥmaṇa baiṣṇaba haityā kaila pāpamati //
brāḥmaṇa baiṣṇabera himsā dekhibāre nāri /
eteka kahiyā tabe rūsilā saṅkari // 3
bhairabi jogini jata nikaṭe chila /
joḍahasta kairā tārā chamute ḍāṛāila //
tabe durgā kahe suna jateka bhairabi /
bhāskarake bāma haiñā nabāke sadaya habi // 4
eteka baliyā durgā karilā gamana /
ekhana jerūpe bhāskara maila śuna bibarana // 5

1. Mustaphi reads /strī puruṣa/.
2. Mustaphi reads /dekhi/.
3. Mustaphi reads /śaṅkarī/.
4. The fourth word in the line is a clear scribal error for /nabābake/.
5. Mustaphi reads /jerupete/.

When Bhāskara Paṇḍit returned to Kāṭañā, the Nabāb heard of it and pitched his camp at Monakarā. Men were being enlisted for his army and there was noise and excitement in the town, and merchants and shopkeepers accompanied the Nabāb. There was a mustering of troops at Monakarā.[120] Hear now of Bhāskara.

Āli Bhāi [121] said to Bhāskara:

—How many more times will you come [to Bengal] in this way? Order the army to refrain from looting the villages. I shall go and arrange for you to meet with the Nabāb.

Bhāskara replied:

—Go then and meet him. But be wary.

So, taking with him twenty-five horsemen, Āli went to Monakarā to meet the Nabāb. When he came to Phuṭisāko, Āli Bhāi stopped and sent a messenger. The messenger came to the Nabāb and said to him:

—Āli Bhāi has come, and he seeks an audience with the Nabāb Sāheb.

And the Nabāb said:

—Tell him to leave his weapons and come to me.

120. The meaning here is obscure. It may also mean that Bhāskara came to Kāṭwā learning that the Nawāb had encamped at Monkarā. The third line in MS may also be read *pal cāi.*

121. Āli Bhāi Qarawal, a Maratha officer who had embraced Islam. Salīm (p. 347) has:

"Mahabat Jang . . . diplomatically established friendly relations with Ali Qarawal, who was one of the Mahratta leaders who had embraced the Muhammadan faith, and was surnamed Ali Bhai. From considerations of expediency, Mahabat Jang invited him over. Receiving him kindly and courteously . . . he made him consent to arrange an interview between himself and Bhaskara. . . ."

ukila āsiñā tabe kahilena tāke /
hātiyāra thuiyā jāiñā mila nabābake //
āli bhāi yāilā tabe hātiyāra thuiyā /
pacisa ghoḍā śuddhā milila āsiyā //
nabāba bole tumi āilā ki kārana / 1
āli bhāi bole bandabastera kārana //
bhāskarera sāthe bibada kene kara /
dui janāte miilā kichu bandabasta kara //
tabe nabāba sāheba bulilena tāre /
bhāskara yāsiñā nākī milibe āmāre //
je samae purbbe gheirāchila baddamāne /
se ṣamae ukila āmī pāṭhāilâū tāra sthāne //
bandabasta karite jadi thākita tāra mane /
sei samae ukila pāṭhāita āmāra sthāne //
muluka poḍāila luṭila bārabāra /
kiu(w)āra saṅge bandabasta kariba yāra //
āli bhāi bole jāhā habāra tā haila /
kadācita ukathā mukhe āra nā buila //
dui saradāra tumi deha yāmāra sane /
bhāskarake milāiyā āni ei sthāne //
tabe nabāba sāheba kahila dujanāre /
āli bhāiera saṅge jāiyā āna bhāskare //

1. Last word in the line unclear in MS.

So Jānakīrām and Mustaphā Khān went to Kāṭañā and met with Bhāskara. Āli Bhāi said to Bhāskara:

—Mustaphā Khān and Jānakīrām have come, sent by the Nabāb. They will conduct you there and arrange for a meeting.

When he heard this, Mir Habib said:

—It is not right that Bhāskara should go.

And to Bhāskara he said:

—You must not go to him. Do you know what the Mogāl's intention is? Hear me, O Bhāskara—do not go.

But Mustaphā Khān said:

—Why do you say these things? We two shall take him with us, and when the agreement has been made, we shall conduct him back to this place. If you doubt me, I take an oath on the Korān.[123]

And Jānakīrām said:

—And I, by the water of the Ganges and the *śālagrāma*;[124] swear that we shall return him to you.

When he heard this Bhāskara said:

—It is good.

Mustaphā Khān said:

—Then let us depart quickly.

123. Salīm (p. 348) says: "Mustafā K͟hān had with him, under a cover, a brick instead of the *Qorān*, and holding it he repeated oaths."

124. *Śālagrāma* is a small, black, and round stone, emblem of Viṣṇu, found in the Bandaki River near a village called Śālagrām. By touching the water of the Ganges and the *śālagrāma*, Jānakīrām took the most sacred oath possible for a Hindu.

jānakīrāma mustaphā khā̃ dui jana calila /
kāṭoñāe jāiñā bhāskarake milila //
bhāskarake āli bhāi kahite lāgila /
mūstapha khā̃ jānakirāma dui janāe āila //
nabāba sāheba pāṭhāila dui janāre /
saṅge kairā laiyā jāiyā milāre tomāre // 1
eteka suniñā̃ tabe mira habiba kae /
kadācita bhāskarake jāite mata nae //
mira habiba kīchu tabe kahe bhāskare /
kadācita jāiyā tumi nā mila tāhāre //
mogolera phera tumi kīraba manasubā / 2
āmāra kathā suna jadi kadācita nā jābā //
tabe mustaphā khā̃ kahite lāgilā /
eteka kathā tumi kene kahilā //
āmarā dui janāe tabe saṅge kairā niba /
bandabasta kairā puna eikhāne āniba //
kīchu kintu jadi mane karo tumi /
korāna daramāna kairā kīrā khāichi āmi // 3
jānakīrāma kahe gaṅgā sālagrāma chuiyā / 4
kichu cintā nāi tomāke yāniba milāiyā //
eteka suniñā bhāskara bole bhāla$_2$ /
mustaphā khā̃ bole tabe sigra kaira cala /

1. Folio ends after /jāiyā/.
2. Mustaphi reads /karibā/; the scribe is probably in error.
3. Mustaphi reads /thāichi/; scribal error is possible.
4. Mustaphi reads /gaṅgājala/, which is incorrect; the last word in the line is unclear in MS: Mustaphi reads /laiyā/.

Bhāskara said:

—How many men shall I take with me?

Jānakīrām said:

—Take as many as you like.

But Āli Bhāi said:

—There is no need for a force. Take ten or twelve men with you.

And Bhāskara, as if afflicted with the madness of the time of death, was deluded by the words of Āli Bhāi, and set off. It was Śukrabār, the first day of Baiśākh when Bhāskara went forth to meet the Nabāb. He went with Āli Bhāi and others, twenty-two men in all. He pitched his camp at night at Palāsi, and the next day set forth. Now hear what the Nabāb did.

As the messenger announced that Bhāskara was approaching, the Nabāb convened his court. Sotābardār Khān[125] sat before the Nabāb, and all around him were the great *jamādārs*. It was on Śanibār[126] the second of Baiśākh that they brought Bhāskara to the Nabāb's place. Fate was against Bhāskara, and had befuddled his mind. He laid aside his weapons and went to meet the Nabāb.

125. Sotābardār Khān may be the name of a person, but, if so, would be unusual. "*Sotābardār*" literally means a macebearer or staffbearer.

126. Saturday.

bhāskara bole sāthe pha͠uja niba kata /
jānakīrāma bole tomāra mone laya jata //
āli bhāi bole pha͠ujera nāhi kāma /
janā dasa bāro loka saṅge kairā jāna //
mirttakāla haile jena matichatte pāe / 1
āli bhāiera kathāe bhāskara bhuilā jāe //
prathama baisākha māsa śukrabāra dine /
bhāskara calila milite nabābera sane //
āli bhāi ādi kari bāisa janā yāila /
palāsi yāsiñā bhāskara serāe thākila // 2
tāra paradine bhāskara karilā gamana /
ethā nabāba laiñā kichu śuna bibarana //
harakārā bole nabābake bhāskara yāise /
eteka suniñā nabāba sabhā kairā baise //
soṭābarddāra khā saraddāra nabābera āge /
baṛa baṛa jamādāra basilā cāiradige //
dusarañi baisākha māsa śanibāra dine /
bhāskarake laiyā āila nabābera sthāne //
bidhātā bipatya haila budhya guilā gela / 3
hātiyāra thuiyā āisā nabāke milila //

1. Mustaphi reads /maticchanna/.
2. Mustaphi reads /ḍerāya/.
3. The last three words in the line are very difficult to read in MS.

When Bhāskara Paṇḍit met the Nabāb, the Nabāb said:
—You have ravaged my kingdom time and time again. Then you sent Āli Bhāi to me to ask for peace. There was a time when you had surrounded Barddhamān. I sent a messenger to you then. If you had wanted to make peace, that was the time when it should have been made.

Then Āli Bhāi said:
—That which has been has been. Now Bhāskara is here; grant him something—give way a little. Make peace with him.

When he heard this, the Nabāb smiled and said:
—Wait for me here. I must go outside and relieve myself.[127]

There was an understanding between the Nabāb and his courtiers. Now, as part of the plan, the Nabāb arose and went out. He was gone a long time. Finally Bhāskara said to Mustaphā:
—I have waited too long.[128] I must go now to my bath and my worship.

Mustaphā Khān replied:
—Let us all go, then. We shall return again in the third watch and see the Nabāb.

127. The text reads: *laghyi kairā āsi*, a polite form of saying urinate.
128. The text says literally, "I have waited for two *ḍaṇḍas*." A *ḍaṇḍa* is about twenty-four minutes, the sixtieth part of a day.

bhāskara paṇḍita jadi milu nabābake /
tāra pare nabāba kahena kichu tāke //
āmāra muluka tumi luṭīlā bāre$_2$ /
bandabasta karite pāṭhāilā āli bhāiera tare //
je kāle āsiñā tumi gherilā barddamāne /
se śamae ukila āmī pāṭhāilāu tomāra sthāne //
bandabasta karite jadi thākita tomāra mone /
sei samae ukila tumi pāṭhāitā āmāre sthāne //
tabe eteka suniñā bhāi āli kahila /
eta dina jāhā habāra tāhā haila //
bhāskara paṇḍita jadi milu tomāra sthāne / 1
kichu diñā̃ bandabasta kara ihāra sane //
eteka suniñā nabāba kahilena hāsi /
khānika bilamba kara laghyi kairā āsi // 2
purbbe sabhāri manasubā chila /
sei manasubāe nabāba uṭhā gela //
nabāba uṭhiyā gela haila anekakṣana /
bhāskara paṇḍita kīchu kahena takhana // 3
dui ḍaṇḍa bilamba haila kahe mustaphāra ṭhāi /
ekhana tabe āmi śrāna pujāe jāi // 4
mustaphā khā̃ bole calo sabhāi milā jāi /
se paharite āsiba nabābera ṭhāi //

1. The last three words in the line are unclear; Mustaphi reads /mile/ and /sane/.
2. The fourth word in the line is unclear.
3. The lasts two words are illegible; the reading is Mustaphi's.
4. Mustaphi reads /sāna/.

So saying, Mustaphā Khān arose. Seeing him rise, Bhāskara rose also. And as Bhāskara was about to mount his horse he was struck with a sword.[129]

A great tumult arose, and all [the Bargis] who came were killed. And when the Nabāb heard the news, he was delighted. Joyful music began to play, and alms were distributed to fakirs and to the poor.

So Bhāskara was killed at Monakarā camp, and Gaṅgārām has fulfilled his wish and told the story.

Here ends the first part of the *Mahārāṣṭa-purāṇa*, the *Bhāskara-parābhaba*, dated *sakābdā* 1672, *sana* 1158 *sāla*, 14 *pouṣ*, the day *śanibār*.

129. There are slightly variant versions of the assassination in Yusuf 'Ali (*Bengal Nawābs*, pp. 108-109), Salīm (pp. 348-349), and Ghulām Hussain (Vol. I, pp. 433-436). As an example, Yusuf 'Ali's version is like this:

"The day of the interview having been fixed, one day before it the Nawāb pitched a lofty tent with spacious screens (*kanāt*) forming a long courtyard; [he] informed Saulat Jang, Mir Muhammad J'afar Khān, Faqirullah Beg Khān, and other generals of his secret plan, and ordered them to place his brave soldiers, fully armed, in two or three rows close together inside the screens, to wait for his order; and when the Nawāb would give the signal, they should instantly and without the least delay carry out the plan with utmost bravery, so that after the design had been executed they might be rewarded in various ways. All the soldiers, on hearing this order, girt their loins to do the work. Next morning, which was to prove the evening of the life of Bhāskara, 'Alivardi went and sat down in the (tent) and waited for the arrival of the prey . . . when Ghulām Mustafā Khān, Jānaki Rām, and Ali Bhāi arrived with Bhāskara and the other chiefs of the Marathas. . . . First the Maratha generals entered the screened tent and stood in a line. As one of them entered, 'Alivardi enquired, 'Is he Rāoji?' 'til Bhāskara, hand in hand with Jānaki Rām, came in. . . . Just then the Nawāb cried in a loud voice, 'Slay all these infidels.' Immediately on hearing it the blood-drinking heroes unsheathed their swords and turned their faces to the infidels and reddened the earth of the field with the blood of the Deccani *sardārs* in a twinkle of an eye. Bhāskara was slain with 19 of his generals."

eteka buliyā mustaphā khā̃ uṭhila /
tāhāra dekhale tabe bhāskara uṭhila //
jei mātra bhāskara ghoḍāe caḍite /
talaāra khuliyā takhana mārileka tāthe //
seikṣane tabe ghaṭāraṭṭi haila / 1
jata janā yāisā chila saba janā maila //
tāra pare nabāba sāheba samācāra śune /
suni yānandita nabāba hailā seikṣane // 2
sādiyānā nahabata kata bājite lāgila / 3
phakira phukurāke khaerāta kata dila //
monakarā mokāme jadi bhāskara maila /
manasubāda uṛāiyā kabi gaṅgārāma kaila //

* * * * *

iti māhārāṣṭa pūrāne prathama kāṇḍe bhāskara parābhaba sakābda 1672 sana 1158 sāla tārikha 14 pouṣa roja sanibāra

1. Mustaphi reads /ghaṭācaṭṭi/.
2. /suniyā ānandita/?
3. The third word in the line is illegible; this is Mustaphi's reading.

APPENDIX I

The Madanamohana-bandanā

Introduction

One of the most curious lines in the text of the *Mahārāshṭā Purāṇa* is that which reads: "But Gopāl defended Bonabiṣṇupur and defeated the Bargis, and against him the Bargis could do nothing." [1] The reigning king of Vishnupur at the time of the Maratha raids was Gopāl Singh. But the allusion is to the presiding deity of Vishnupur—Gopāl, a name of Kṛṣṇa or Madanamohana. The poet might have intended a play on the word Gopāl. The story is recounted below:

In the first part of the sixteenth century there was a king of Vishnupur named Vīra Hamvīra, who had been converted to Vaiṣṇavism by some of the disciples of Caitanya [2] and had had constructed an image of Madanamohana (one of the names of Kṛṣṇa, also called Gopāl). His descendant, Gopāl Singh (1730-45), was the ruler of Vishnupur during the Bargi incursions.

"He was a pious prince, whose memory is held in veneration to this day by the people of Bishnupur. It was characteristic of this Rājā that he issued an edict that all the people of Mallabhūm should count their beads and repeat the name of God (Harinām) [3] every evening at sunset. . . . But his religious zeal was not supported by military prowess. During his reign the Marathas under Bhāskar Rāo appeared before the southern gate of Bishnupur, and after the troops had made a spirited sally, Gopāl Singh retreated inside the fort and ordered both soldiers and citizens to join in prayers to the god of his family to save the city. This prayer was heard, and legend relates, the guns were fired without human assistance by the god Madan Mohan. The truth probably is that the Maratha cavalry were unable to pierce the strong fortifications

1. See translation, p. 34.
2. See the *Narottama-vilāsa* of Narahari-dāsa (Murshidabad: Rādhā-ramaṇa Press, 1328 B. S. [A. D. 1922]), pp. 34-35.
3. A chant used by Vaiṣṇavas, literally, name of the god Hari (Kṛṣṇa).

and retired, leaving the Rājā's levies to plunder their abandoned camp." [4]

The text which relates the story of the image of Vishnupur is called the *Madanamohana-bandanā.* It was written probably in the eighteenth century by Jayakṛṣṇadāsa. The manuscript of the work which we have is dated 1267 B.S. (A.D. 1861). But whatever the date of the text itself, it seems clear that the legend of Madanamohana and the Bargis goes back to an earlier time.

An extract from the *Madanamohana-bandanā* is given in Dinesh Chandra Sen's *Vaṅga sāhitya paricaya* (Calcutta University, 1914), Vol. II, pp. 1416-1421. The relevant part of that extract is translated below.

Translation

From that day forth we were delivered [from all danger] by your grace, [O Lord]. For even when the Bargis had surrounded the fort,[5] they were not able to plunder it because of your intercession.

One day the people were gathered together in one place, chanting the name of God; and they said to the king:

—Hear us, O king! Why do you sit there idly? We have come to ask you to drive off the Bargis.

And the king answered:

—Hear me, my people. I have not the power to do this. But Madanamohana will drive them off.

When they heard these words, the people were astonished, and they said:

—The *mahārājā* says that Madanamohana will drive off the Bargis!

The Bargis had assembled all their forces together in one place. They passed the four *ghāṭs* [6] and advanced to the *yuja-ghāṭ.*[7] Many

4. *Bengal District Gazetteer, Bankura,* p. 28.

5. The text has "for twelve years" (*bāra batsara*). This is a pious exaggeration, for while Maratha incursions into Bengal continued sporadically for a much longer time, Bhāskara, to whom this text specifically refers, invaded Bengal in A.D. 1742 and was killed in 1744.

6. The term "*ghāṭ*" denotes a pass of some kind. Some *ghāṭs* were hill-passes in the strict sense of the term, but others merely embraced a section of an ordinary road, and others again nothing but areas of open country, which might contain one or more villages and might not be traversed by any road

Bargis descended into the ditch of Talabaruja,[8] and mounted upon elephants. A gunner then ran and went to Dakṣinabhadra [9] and made this complaint to the king:
—Hear, O king. Why do you sit there idly? I have come to ask you to drive off the Bargis.

When he heard these words, the king began to tremble in fear, and he called to him all the *kīrtanīyas* [10] of the city. They went to the temple-precincts [11] of Mahāprabhu [12] and began their *kīrtan.*
—Protect us, O Madanamohana!

Thus the king prayed in a loud voice. And Madanamohana was in that place, and he knew these things in his heart:
—The king and his people have laid this obligation upon me—that I drive out the Bargis.

Then the Lord put on his battle-dress,[13] and, beautiful, went forth through the Śākhāri-bājār to drive out the Bargis.[14] When the people of the Śākhāri-bājār saw his horse, they all ran after it to catch it. But who could catch that horse, with the Lord mounted upon its back? And the horse stopped when it reached the *yuja-ghāṭ.* And there Bhāskara Paṇḍit, the general of the Bargis, saw him. And when [Bhāskara] saw his form like a mountain, the true form of Yama. . . .[15] And when they saw these things, the Bargis fled away. Then the Lord dismounted and, taking a match in his

at all. There was " a quasi-military body of men " called " *ghatuals* " employed for the protection of *ghāṭs.* " *Ghāṭ* " also means a landing place on a river.

7. The form " *yuja* " is an old Bengali form of " *yuddha,*" battle.
8. *Talburu* refers to a tower in the rampart; the ditch mentioned refers to the moat round the fort. " Palm Tower " (*talburu*) is so called probably because of its height.
9. A name for a place in or around the city.
10. " Those who perform *kīrtan.*" *Kīrtan* refers to a Vaiṣṇava form of worship with songs of praise and sometimes ecstatic dancing.
11. The term used is *beṛe.* Its meaning is " an enclosed place, precinct."
12. " Great Lord "—the term is frequently used to refer to Caitanya.
13. Literally, the dress of a wrestler—*mallabeśa.*
14. *Śākhāri-bājār* is " the market-place of those who work with conch shells," i. e., those who sell conches for ritual purposes, who make bangles of them, etc.; a part of the town.
15. Yama is the god of death and punishment, the guardian of Hell. There is a gap in the text at this point. Sen gives no indication as to whether it is a hiatus in the MS or whether he has omitted a section in his printed text.

hand, put it to the cannon. The Bargis fled, and their elephants were killed.

When the news of the flight of the Bargis came to the king, he said:

—Who fired the guns against my orders?

And all the gunners said:

—We do not know. We were at our own positions, and only heard the sound.

But one gunner pondered and said:

—When the guns were fired, I thought I smelled the sweet scent of Kṛṣṇa's body.

When he heard this, the king began to tremble in ecstasy.

—Ah, wretch that I am; Kṛṣṇa did not show himself to me!

And when he had said this the king began to dance. He danced to the temple of the Lord. He opened the door and looked around. There was sweat dripping from the body of Madanamohana. There was gunpowder on his hands, and the dust of the field was on his feet. And when he saw this, the king ran forth in great joy.

larwaris by 'caste,' [the Seths] traveled from western and central India, ees to commerce, and its pioneers. By religion they were Jains and in 'ounders of the Jain community which is now so largely represented in ;anj. . . . The home of the 'Jaggat Seths' ancestors was in Nagar near ur. About 1695, Hira Nand Sahu, the stock from which our Seths claim t, stirred by the migratory impulse which drives every Marwari to try ck in new centers of commerce, began his travels. When Hira Nand s far as Patna he was attracted by that bustling city and its great . This pioneer of the Seths was not long before he had amassed a con-ble fortune which left him with few rivals in Patna. Fortune must have avoured him in the choice of a wife. This lady bore him seven sons, ll seven, when they arrived at manhood, became bankers, scattering elves over India.

e son whose career is of interest to us was Manick Chand. He settled cca, then the capital of Bengal and the home of the Nawab ruling as of Bengal, Bihar, and Orissa. Thus it remained until 1704. In that Murshid Kuli Khan made Muxsudabad his capital, changing the name, have seen, to Murshidabad. Naturally enough Manick Chand moved he court. He is said to have been in favour with Murshid Kuli Khan, romoted the Seth to be one of his advisors as well as his banker. . . . tle 'Seth' was conferred upon the Marwari by Furrakshah in 1715. . . . k Chand, having no son, adopted a nephew, one Fateh Chand Seth, artner in a firm in Delhi. The Emperor was under many obligations firm, so that there was no difficulty in obtaining for the adopted son sition of trust, formerly filled by Manick Chand, who died in A. D. 1722. aid that when Fateh Chand established himself in Murshidabad he was hest man in India.

e title 'Jaggat Seth' ('banker of the world') was conferred on Fateh at his first visit to the Emperor Mahomed Shah, in 1724. . . . When 1-Dowlah succeeded Murshid Kuli Khan in 1728, Fateh Chand was his four councillors. Fateh Chand found favor with each ruling Nawab, e succession of Serfiraz Khan in 1739 made no change in his position. breach occurred was due, it is said, to the lust of the Nazim, who, of the great beauty of the wife of Fateh Chand's son, sought to see . Jaggat Seth, burning with hatred toward his oppressor, entered into nication with Ali Verdi Khan. Carried back to honour and power after ccessful revolt of Ali Verdi Khan, Fateh Chand lived in luxury until when he died. . . ." (Pp. 254-255.)

story of the insult visited upon the house of Jagat Seth is mentioned ne contemporaries and is a common story in Bengal. But it may or ot be true. Dr. Jadunath Sarkar (*History of Bengal*, Vol. II, p. 439)

king advantage of the weakness of Sarfaraz, Alivardi and Haji Ahmad rmed the design of seizing the government of Bengal. . . . They were secure the friendship of a prominent official of the Nawab's *darbar*, and, and that of Jagat Seth Fatehchand, whose changed attitude s the son of the deceased Nawab was due more to their desire to his distracted situation to their own advantage than to any other There is no reliable evidence for asserting that the Nawab, though a

APPENDIX II

Footnote 20, p. 10: Yusuf 'Ali (Sarkar, *Bengal Nawābs*, p. 96) has: "Bhāskara, after passing through the wilderness (jungles) by way of the hills of Orissa, wished to enter Bengal, but finding no way on that side, turned to the pass of Pachet, which is eight marches west of Murshidabad. 'Alivardi, learning this news at Jhinkara, at first did not give credit to the report. . . . The path for entering the kingdom had . . . been confined to the well-known route by the pass of Sikrigali."

The *Riyāẓu-s-salāṯīn* of G͟hulām Husain Salīm (Zaidpūrī), translated by Maulavi Abdūs Salām (Calcutta: Asiatic Society, 1902), gives a similar account, and the translator writes (p. 338, note 1) that:

"It is related in the *Seiru-l-Mutakherin* (Persian text, p. 507), whose author's father, Syed Hedair Khān, was at the time employed as Faujdar of Magha in Behar and was on an expedition to the hill-passes of Ramgarh, that the Mahratta cavalry numbering 40,000, led by Bhāskar Paṇḍit, general of Raghoji Bhoslah, swooped down through the above passes, cut through Pachit and Morbhanj, and appeared on the outskirts of Mednīpur."

Footnote 33, p. 18: Yusuf 'Ali says: "'Alivardi, after his return from Katak, as he had no anticipation of trouble in any direction, and saw no man as probable enemy, had dismissed many troops, and now had not more than five or six thousand cavalry with him; many of these too had taken the road to Murshidabad, thinking that there was no danger on the way and that the army was coming (soon) to Murshidabad; so that 'Alivardi was accompanied by not more than three or four thousand cavalry and four or five thousand infantry of the topkhanah. . . ." (*Bengal Nawābs*, p. 96.)

Yusuf 'Ali says that it was the Nawāb who promised money to his troops. "Instead of giving this money to the enemy under such humiliation, it is better that, God willing, after fighting the battle I shall pay ten lakhs of rupees as reward to the faithful soldiers. . . ." (*Bengal Nawābs*, p. 98.)

Footnote 47, p. 22: Salīm says: "The hungry troops, who for three days and nights had not seen . . . foodstuffs, quenched the fire of their hunger with the stores of Burdwan. The army of Marhatta freebooters followed up in pursuit. Sacking villages and towns of the surrounding tracts, and engaging in slaughter and capture, they set fire to granaries and spared no vestige of fertility. And when the stores and granaries of Burdwan were exhausted, and the supply of imported grains was also completely cut off, to avert death by starvation human beings ate plantain roots, whilst the animals were fed on the leaves of the trees. Even these gradually ceased to be available. For breakfast and supper, nothing but the discs of the sun and the moon feasted their eyes. And for days and nights together, being constantly mounted on their high saddles, they did not even dream of sleep."

Footnote 51, p. 24: Yusuf 'Ali relates it in this way (*Bengal Nawābs*, p. 97):

"According to this design he rode out in the morning, issuing strict orders to his troops to leave their baggage (*bahir*) on the camping ground and not to allow the (camp followers) to join the fighting column. But the camp people, in fear of the Marathas, did not listen to him and forced their way into the column of soldiers."

Footnote 52, p. 24: Salīm (p. 337) has Mīr Ḥabīb playing a much more instrumental part in the whole affair: " Mīr Ḥabīb, the Generalissimo of Murshīd Qulī K͟hān [i. e., Rastam Jang], after the latter's defeat, had gone to Raghojī Bhonslah, and had persuaded the latter to undertake the conquest of Bengal. . . . Raghojī detached Diwan Bhāskar Paṇḍit and Alī Qarawāl, who was an able general, with a contingent of sixty thousand Mahratta cavalry, in the company of Mīr Ḥabīb . . . to invade and pillage Bengal."

Footnote 55, p. 24: Salīm (p. 339) names him as "Muṣāḥib K͟hān Mohmand, son of U'mar K͟hān the General," and the translation points out in a note that the name indicates that he was an Afghan of the Mohmand clan. Salīm's text (p. 339), and Salimullah (p. 107) have a more detailed and colorful version of the death of Mosaheb Khān. Salīm says:

"The Mahrattas at once hemming in attacked the elephant Landāh on which Mahābat Jang's Begam was mounted, and capturing the elephant dragged it toward their own camp. Muṣāḥib K͟hān Mohmand . . . having his Hindustānī courage aroused in him, attacked the freebooters and, advancing in valour and gallantry, by means of valourous onslaughts and Rustam-like onsets, rescued the elephant together with its fair rider from the clutches of the freebooters. In consequence, however, of the numerous mortal and ghastly wounds that they received, Muṣāḥib K͟hān and a large number of his comrades and kinsmen drew the red paint of martyrdom on their faces, and on that very spot of slaughter were buried."

Footnote 59, p. 26: Yusuf 'Ali's text (p. 100) has: "On this day all the remaining baggage and belongings of our army were plundered by the enemy, and nothing remained of our surplus baggage, nay, of the necessary articles of food, clothing, and conveyance. [We had only] two or three thousand men on horses and some on elephants, and five or six thousand men on foot. Fighting in this manner, and marching from dawn to evening prayer, we halted at sunset on the bank of a water [?—tank or river?], where for high and low alike nothing was available as cover except the shadow of the heavens or as bed except the bare ground. As for food, for the men accustomed to comfort, not once in the day or night was anything found to allay their hunger; as for the common people, they filled their stomachs by eating the stalk of the banana plant [*sāq-i-shajar-manz*] and similar things. The [present] author had gone to meet his father on the way in the company of the Nawab during this journey. I remember that on the third day I obtained one quarter seer of *khichri,* which was shared by seven persons, while three other men lived on seven pieces of *shakar-parah*, which is a kind of sweetmeat. . . . On the day of reaching Katwa the hungry men, under the belief that abundance of grain of all kinds would be found there, arrived there with utmost possible speed. But the fact was that the Marathas had entered it before our arrival, plundered the village, and set fire to the granaries of rice which they could not carry away. In this way men and beasts fasted for three days. On the fourth day,

on reaching Katwa, they fed upon the bur

It is interesting that this account sound
Nawāb's suffering, which in his version h
of such texts were not often careful abou

Salīm, again, agrees essentially with Ga
but adds some interesting details:

"It was at last decided to place the a
the baggage in the center, and in this for
Burdwan to Katwah, where food and foo
could be imported by waterways from
relieve the distressed soldiery. In short,
out at night from Burdwan, Mahabat Jan
The light Mahratta cavalry, however, co
is about two miles] * a day, and thus before
they had already burnt down its fields,
them to ashes. . . . However, Hāji Āhm
shidabad, got breads prepared, and sent
and foodstuffs on boats to Katwah. . . ."

* The Persian text (*Riyāẓu-s-salāṭīn* of G
Asiatic Society, 1890-1898), p. 342, says li
the foe, swift as the wind, would travel fo

Footnote 79, p. 34: Yusuf 'Ali again differs (p
to Hugli and captured Muhammad Yār B
who was posed there as the deputy of the
collectors in Hugli and Hijli."

Salīm (p. 342; Persian text, p. 344) give
years Mīr Ḥabīb had lived at Hugli, the lat
of his kinsmen and friends. Their headman,
plans to surprise Hugli. He won over man
held secret correspondence with Mīr Ḥabīb.
of Mīr Abu-l-Ḥasan, Mīr Ḥabīb with a de
commanded by Sis Rao advanced to Hugli
gate of its Fort, announced his arrival to
influence of liquor the Deputy Faujdār unh
Fort to be thrown open and to admit Mī
Sis Rao with his cavalry entered the Fort. M
were Mīr Ḥabīb's acquaintances were intro
The Rāo treated them courteously and defer
tions of peace and security and forbade the
the town."

Footnote 90, p. 36: Salīm (p. 342) has: "Hājī
and Ḥusain Qulī K͟hān, who were in the city,
cavalry, firing their guns once or twice and
well as the gates of the Citadel, entrenched t
to fight and disperse the enemy, or to defen

Footnote 91, p. 36: The following account is tak
bad District, by Major J. H. Tull Walsh (I
date of Preface, 1902):

dissipated youth, ever took any direct step, calculated to tarnish the honour of the two brothers."

The story of the plunder of Jagat Seth's residence in Murshidabad is also mentioned in *Siyār-ul-Mutākherīn*. The following extract from N. K. Sinha's *Economic History of Bengal* (Vol. I, p. 140), will be of interest:

"Ghulam Hussain does not mention the exact amount of the capital of the Seths but he gives us a very good idea in an indirect way. When the Marathas, guided by Mir Habib, led a lightning raid into Murshidabad in 1742, they succeeded in plundering their *Kothee* and carried away two krores (three lakhs according to Karam Ali) of Arcot rupees. But this did not affect them more than if it had been two trusses of straw. Even after this they continued to give the government bills payable at sight—darshanis— of one crore at a time."

Footnote 92, p. 36. The following is from Sinha's *Economic History of Bengal*, Vol. I, p. 119:

"The Arcot rupees were originally struck by the Nawab of Arcot, but the English, the French and the Dutch also received the privilege of coining in Madras, Pondicherry and Nagapatam, and English, French and Dutch Arcots also poured into Bengal. . . . Mandeville, who was in Bengal in 1750, gives a list of coins he found in trading circles in Calcutta in 1750—*Sicca* rupees, Arcot rupees and Ely (Patna) rupees. 'All these rupees do (or ought to) weigh ten massa weight but then they differ in fineness or touch. The Bengal Sicca rupee is best of all . . . the Arcot rupee is commonly bad and light and the Ely rupee still worse'."

Footnote 93, p. 36: The following is an excerpt from *Riyāẓu-s-Salātīn* (pp. 339-340):

"And when the freebooters from impudence and insolence made onslaughts from all sides, Mahabat Jung ['Alivardi Khan], of necessity, opened leathern bags of coins, and scattered them on the field. Thus diverting the freebooters with the work of picking up coins, Mahabat Jung seized this respite, and with the celerity of lightning and wind, riding out at full gallop, arrived at Bardwan."

By this time the Marathas had extended their control over a large part of western Bengal. Yusuf 'Ali (*Bengal Nawābs*, pp. 101-102) has:

"The entire *chakla* of Burdwan was taken possession of by the Marathas, and they occupied Medinipur up to Bālesar. . . . The *zila* of Birbhum, many of the *parganas* of Rajshahi, the city of Rājmahal, also fell into Maratha hands. Nothing remained in the Nawāb's hands except the city of Murshidabad and the country on this side of the Ganges, namely Dacca, Rangpur, etc."

Footnote 105, p. 44: Yusuf 'Ali (in *Bengal Nawābs*, p. 104) says:

"Safdar Jang, under orders of the Emperor to aid 'Alivardi, came from his province of Oudh to Patna, treated the people of that city with great haughtiness and insolence, and . . . took away some guns and two choice elephants of Zainuddin Ahmad Khan, who was at that time in the company of his uncle in the campaign against the Marathas."

Safdar Jang's expedition is not mentioned by Gaṅgārām. It is obvious that the Emperor of Delhi did not follow a consistent policy.

Footnote 113, p. 50: Yusuf 'Ali (*Bengal Nawābs*, pp. 105-107) outlines these events in the following way: "When Bhāskara came (back) to the Deccan, defeated and broken, Raghuji on hearing of it assembled his army and with Bhāskara set out for Bengal. At the same time Bālā Rāo Pandit, the son of the celebrated Bāji Rāo, one of the pillars of the Maratha state, started for Bengal by way of Bunkelkhand, by order of the Emperor, for collecting a *tankha* (assignment) of fifteen lakhs of rupees from the revenue of Bengal and for expelling Raghuji from that country. . . . Raghu by the route of the jungles of Birbhum and Bālā Rāo by the frequented public road, set out for Bengal. Raghu, having reached Bengal before Bālā Rāo's arrival, took post between Katwa and Burdwān, and sent Bhāskara with a strong force to Medinipur, and soon afterwards Bālā Rāo . . . following a deserted path, alighted near Mankara. Alivardi was at the same time encamped with his vast army on the bank of the same river. The inhabitants of Murshidabad, in extreme perplexity and terror at the arrival of two such Maratha armies, fell into plans for going out of the city. . . . After the arrival of Bālā Rāo near his own army, 'Alivardi paid him a visit. Bālā Rāo advanced to welcome him and took him into his own tent. . . . The next day Bālā Rāo returned the visit. . . . Raghuji, who was staying between Katwa and Burdwān, on learning of this union and seeing it impossible for himself to fight the enemy, set out for the jungles in the west side of Bengal. Next day, according to the agreement, the two vast armies of Light and Darkness [i. e., 'Alivardi and Bālā Rāo] moved in pursuit of Raghu. . . . After one or two marches, Bālā Rāo asked the Nawāb to let him depart, saying that the Nawāb's army could not march as quickly as was necessary for overtaking Raghu. After sending this message *and taking the assignment of money* [italics ours], Bālāji next day set out . . . and fought and defeated Raghu. . . . Bhāskara, who had gone to Medinipur, on hearing this news, went out through the mountain passes of Orissa in extreme bewilderment. . . . 'Alivardi returned to Murshidabad, this time victorious without having had to undergo the hardships of war."

The text goes on (pp. 107-108): "As described before, the defeated Bhāskara had gone from Bengal to his own country. Next year Rāghu sent Bhāskara again to Bengal at the head of twenty thousand horsemen to make peace if possible, or else to engage in fighting."

Salīm (pp. 346-347) fills in some of the details of Bhāskara's activities in Orissa, where he says Bhāskara spent "three years in guerilla warfare." There were constant engagements between 'Alivardi's troops and Bhāskara but no major battle, and, Salīm says, "it was hard to decide which side eventually came off the best."

BIBLIOGRAPHY

Bengal District Gazeteers: Bankura (1908) and *Birbhum* (1910) by L. S. S. O'Malley, and *Burdwan* (1910), by J. C. K. Peterson. Calcutta, Office of the Superintendent of Government Printing.

Bolts, William. *Considerations on Indian Affairs.* London: printed for J. Almon *et al.*, 1772.

Bhāratcandra. *Bhāratcandra granthābalī.* Brajendranāth Bandyopādrhyāya and Sajanikānta Dās, eds. Calcutta: Sāhitya pariṣad, 1950.

Dasgupta, J. N. "An Eighteenth Century Bengali Manuscript," *Calcutta Review*, April, 1917.

Datta, K. K. *Alivardi and His Times.* Calcutta: Calcutta University, 1939.

G͟hulām-i-ḥusen salīm. *Riyāẓu-s-salāṭīn.* Persian text. Calcutta: The Asiatic Society, 1890-1898.

G͟hulam Husain Salīm (Zaidpūrī). *Riyāẓu-s-salāṭīn.* Maulavi Abdus Salem, trans. Calcutta: The Asiatic Society, 1902.

Ghulām Hussain Khān. *Siyār-ul-Mutākherīn*, Haji Mustefa, trans. 4 vols. Calcutta, 1901-1902. London: The Oriental Translations Fund of Great Britain and Ireland, No. 32, 1932.

Grierson, Sir George. *Linguistic Survey of India.* Vol. 5. Calcutta: Office of the Superintendent of Government Printing, 1903.

Holwell, J. Z. *India Tract.* London: printed for T. Becket, 1774.

——— *Interesting Historical Events Relative to the Province of Bengal and the Empire of Indostan.* London: printed for T. Becket and T. A. de Hondt, 1766-1771.

Journal of the Department of Letters (University of Calcutta), XX (1930).

Karve, Irawati. *Kinship Organization of India.* Poona: Deccan College, 1953.

Majumdar, Ramesh Chandra, *et al. An Advanced History of India.* London: Macmillan, 1950.

Narahari-dāsa. *Narottama-vilāsa.* Murshidabad: Rādhā-ramaṇa Press, 1328 B.S. (A.D. 1922).

Orme, Robert. *A History of the Military Transactions of the British Nation in Indostan.* 4 vols. London: printed for F. Wingrave, 1803.

Pravasi (Calcutta). XXX (1931), XXXI (1932).

Proceedings of the Indian Historical Records Commission. Calcutta, 1924.

Rennell, James. *A Bengal Atlas, containing Maps of the Theatre of War and Commerce on That Side of Hindoostan.* London: The East India Company, 1781.

Sachs, Curt. *Die Musikinstrumente Indiens und Indonesiens.* Berlin und Leipzig: Vereinigung wissenschaftlicher verleger, 1923.

——— *The History of Musical Instruments.* New York: W. W. Norton, 1940.

Sāhitya pariṣad patrikā (Calcutta). XIII (1908), XIV (1909), and XV (1910).

Salimullah. *A Narrative of the Transactions in Bengal during the Soobahdaries.* A translation by Francis Gladwin of the *Tārikh-i-Bangāla* of Salimullah. Calcutta: Stuart and Cooper, 1788.

Samaddar, J. N. " The Maratha Invasion of Bengal in 1743, as told in the Maharashta Purana," *Bengal Past and Present* (Journal of the Calcutta Historical Society), XXVII, January-March, 1924.

Sambamoorthy, P. *Catalogue of Musical Instruments exhibited in the Government Museum, Madras.* Rev. ed. Madras: Superintendent of Government Printing, 1955.

Sarkar, Jadunath. *Bengal Nawābs.* Calcutta: Asiatic Society, 1952.

———, ed. *History of Bengal,* Vol. II. Dacca: Dacca University, 1948.

——— *Fall of the Mughal Empire.* 4 vols. Calcutta: M. S. Sarkar, 1932-1950.

Sardesai, G. S. *Main Currents of Maratha History.* Bombay: Phoenix, 1949.

Scrafton, Luke. *Reflections on the Government of Indostan.* London: printed for W. Richardson, 1763.

Sen, Dinesh Chandra. *Vaṅga sāhitya paricaya.* 2 vols. Calcutta: Calcutta University, 1914.

Sen, Sukumar. *Bāṅgālār sāhityer itihāsa.* 2nd ed. Vol. I. Calcutta: Modern Book Agency, 1948.

——— *Bhāṣār itibṛtta.* Burdwan: Sāhitya pariṣad, 1957.

——— *History of Bengali Literature.* New Delhi: Sahitya Akademi, 1960.

Sen, Surendranath. *Military System of the Marathas.* Calcutta and Bombay: Orient-Longmans, 1958.

Sinha, N. K. *Economic History of Bengal.* Calcutta: Vol. I by the author, 1956; Vol. II by K. L. Mukopadhyaya, 1962.

Stewart, Charles. *History of Bengal.* London, 1813; 2nd ed., Calcutta: Bangabasi Office, 1910.

Vāṇeśvara Vidyālaṅkāra. *Citracampū.* Rāmācaraṇ Cakravarti, ed. Benares: Harakumar Chakravarti, 1940.

Walsh, Major J. H. Tull. *A History of Murshidabad District.* London: Jarold and Sons, n.d. (date of Preface, 1902).

Wilson, Horace Hayman. *A Glossary of Judicial and Revenue Terms.* Rev. ed. A. C. Ganguli and N. D. Basu, eds. Calcutta: Eastern Law House, 1940.

INDEX

Accounts of the Maratha Invasions of Bengal. *See* contemporary English accounts; Persian Chronicles; *Mahārāshṭa Purāṇa*; *Citracampū*

Āhwāl-i-Mahābat Jang by Yusuf 'Ali: description of, xvii; refers to the instigation of Nizām-ul-Mulk, xvii; mentions Rāghuji Bhonsle, xvii; mentions Bhāskar Paṇḍit, xvii; support of 'Alivardi's legitimacy, xviii; mentions condition of 'Alivardi's army, 72

Āli Bhāi, Maratha Officer: asks Bhāskara to cease atrocities in Bengal, 54; meets 'Alivardi, 56

'Alivardi Khān, Nabāb of Bengal: first battle with Marathas, x; deputy of Shujā-ud-din Khān in Bihar, x; revolt against Sarfarāz Khān, x; campaigns against rebels in Orissa, x; murder of Bhāskara Paṇḍit in 1744, x; treaty with Rāghuji Bhonsle, xi; supported by the Seths, state bankers of Bengal, xviii; legitimacy questioned, xviii, 14; receives ultimatum from Bhāskara, 14; fearlessness of, 16; also called Nabāb Sāheb, 36; night march to Monakarā, 38; berates Hāji Sāheb for cowardice, 38; advances to Tārakpur, 44; routs *bargis* at Tārakpur, 44; calls nephews to aid, 44; advised by Jayandi Āhmad Khān, 44-46; rallies his forces, 48; meets with envoy from Bhāskara, 56; arranges to meet Bhāskara, 56; reminds Bhāskara of his refusal of peace at Bardhamān, 62; dismisses troops on return from Katak, 71

Alivardi and His Times by Kalikinkar Datta: utilization of historical material from *Mahārāshṭa Purāṇa*, xx

Allyvherde Caun, xix. *See* 'Alivardi Khān

Āmaṛa, Gaṅgāji. *See* Bhāskara: *jamādārs* of

Āmoṛa, Kesaji. *See* Bhāskara: *jamādārs* of

Annadāmaṅgal by Bhāratcandra Rāy: use of Maratha invasion of Bengal as subject in poetry, xiv

Asāf Jāh Nizām-ul-Mulk, Regulator of the Mughal Empire: serves as viceroy of the Deccan, xvi; encourages invasion of Bengal, xvi, xvii

Āsālat: battle with Mīr Ḥabīb, 42

Āṣāṛh, June-July, beginning of monsoon: *bargis* checked by, 38

Ātāullā: battle with Mīr Ḥabīb, 42

Bādsā. *See* Muhammad Shāh

Baidyas: flee from Marathas, 26

Baiśākh, 19th of, date of first Maratha attack, about 4th of May, 10

baksi bahaniyā, officer in charge of baggage carriers, 42

Bālāji. *See* Bhāskara: *jamādārs* of

Bālārāo. *See* Bhāskara, *jamādārs* of

Bardhamān: 'Alivardi surprised by Maratha cavalry at, x, 10; city razed by Marathas, 32; villages of district razed by Marathas, 34

bargis: used as a general term for the Maratha soldiery, xiii; mentioned in ballads, xiii; mentioned in nursery rhymes, xiii, xxi; remaining traces of, in Bengal, xxii; number of, with Bhāskara, 12; besiege 'Alivardi, 20; names of, in army of Bhāskara, 20; feared in Bengal, 22, 24, 26, 28, 30, 32, 36; cruelty of, 30, 32; Bengali villages razed by, 32; loot Bengali cities, 36; loot house of Jagat Seṭ, 36; retreat from Tārakpur, 44; discover strategy of Jayandi Āhmad Khān, 50; retreat of, 50; murder the people of Bengal, 52; names of those killed with Bhāskara, 64; 68

Bengal: semi-independence during reign

MONOGRAPHS OF THE ASSOCIATION FOR ASIAN STUDIES

Delmer M. Brown, *editor*

I. Money Economy in Japan: A Study in the Use of Coins. *By Delmer M. Brown.* Yale University Press, 1951. Pp. vii, 128. (OP)

II. China's Management of the American Barbarians: A Study of Sino-American Relations, 1841-1861, with documents. *By Earl Swisher.* Yale University Press. Pp. xxi, 884. (OP)

III. Leadership and Power in the Chinese Community of Thailand. *By G. William Skinner.* Cornell University Press, 1958. Pp. xvii, 363.

IV. Siam Under Rama III, 1824-1851. *By Walter F. Vella.* J. J. Augustin, 1957. Pp. viii, 180. (OP)

V. The Rise of the Merchant Class in Tokugawa Japan, 1600-1868: An Introductory Survey. *By Charles David Sheldon.* J. J. Augustin, 1958. Pp. ix, 206. (OP)

VI. Chinese Secret Societies in Malaya: A Survey of the Triad Society from 1800 to 1900. *By L. F. Comber.* J. J. Augustin, 1959. Pp. viii, 324. (OP)

VII. The Traditional Chinese Clan Rules. *By Hui-chen Wang Liu.* J. J. Augustin, 1959. Pp. x, 264.

VIII. A Comparative Analysis of the Jajmani System. *By Thomas O. Beidelman.* J. J. Augustin, 1959. Pp. xi, 86.

IX. Colonial Labor Policy and Administration. *By J. Norman Parmer.* J. J. Augustin, 1960. Pp. xii, 294.

X. Bangkhuad—A Community Study in Thailand. *By Howard Keva Kaufman.* J. J. Augustin, 1960. Pp. ix, 235.

XI. Agricultural Involution: The Processes of Ecological Change in Indonesia. *By Clifford Geertz.* University of California Press, 1963. Pp. 176.